∆D Ar

The Transformable House

Guest-edited by Jonathan Bell and Sally Godwin

WILEY-ACADEMY

Architectural Design
Vol 70   No 4

ISBN 0-471-49605-7
Profile No 146

Editorial Offices
International House
Ealing Broadway Centre
London W5 5DB
T: +44 (0)20 8326 3800
F: +44 (0)20 8326 3801

Editor
Maggie Toy

Managing Editor
Helen Castle

Production
Mariangela Palazzi-Williams

Art Director
Christian Küsters ↘ CHK Design

Design Assistant
Owen Peyton Jones ↘ CHK Design

Advertisement Sales
01243 843272

Photo Credits
Abbreviated positions
b=bottom, c=centre, l=left, r=right, t=top

ΔD Architectural Design
p 5 Courtesy Katy Ghahremani, © Katy Gahahremani/HangerHouse Company; p 6 courtesy Pierre-Alexandre Coinde, © The Centre of Attention; p 8 © b consultants; p 10 courtesy Hubert-Jan Henket, © Centraal Museum, Utrecht; p 12 photos © Sally Godwin, Schröder House © DACS 2000; p 13 courtesy Hubert-Jan Henket, © Centraal Museum; p 15(l) courtesy Hubert-Jan Henket, © Centraal Museum; p 15(r) photo © Sally Godwin, Schröder House © DACS 2000; pp 16–19 courtesy Design Museum, London; pp 20–25 photos: © Iain Borden; p 23(l) courtesy RIBA Library Photographs Collection; p 26 Janet Hall/RIBA Library Photographs Collection; p 29 (b) RIBA Library Photographs Collection; p 30 RIBA Library Photographs; Collection; p 32 RIBA Library Photographs; Collection; p 35 © James Gallie; p 36 © RUIMTELAB; p 37 © Yona Friedman; p 38 courtesy Spacex Gallery, © Alex Tymko/Spacex Gallery (Spacex Gallery would like to thank the following organisations for supporting the HOMING project: Hesco Bastion Company, Stansell Ltd, Independent Recycling Ltd, Multifoil Ltd, Parker Merchandising, Sumerfield Developments, Brandon Tool Hire, Planning Services, Exeter City Council); pp 40–41 courtesy Maureen Paley, © David Thorpe and Maureen Paley/Interim Art; pp 42–47 © Jestico + Whiles (co-consultant ECD Energy and Environment and Barton Engineers);

p 48 courtesy Massachusetts Institute of Technology; pp 50–51 © Steven Holl Architects; pp 52–57 courtesy Lazzarini Pickering, Monte Carlo photos: © Matteo Piazza and Rome photos: © Giovanna Piemonti; pp 58–61 © Helmut Dippold; pp 62–64 © Mark Guard Architects, photos: Ianthe Ruthven; p 66 © Henry Wilson; pp 68–69 © Mark Guard Architects; p 70(t) © Mark Guard Architects, photo: Allan Mower; p 70(b) © Mark Guard Architects; p 71(t) and p 71(r) © Mark Guard Architects; p 71(bl) © Mark Guard Architects, photo: Alan Williams; pp 72–73 © Cartwright Pickard Architects, photos: Martin Charles; pp 74–75 photos © Paul Smoothy; pp 76–77 photos courtesy Van Berkel and Bos, © Christian Richters; p 78 © Van Berkel and Bos; pp 79–81 photos: © Stephen Varady; pp 82–85 © Softroom Ltd; pp 86–89 photos courtesy Hans Peter Wörndl, © Paul Ott; pp 90–91 photos and renderings: © Richard Murphy Architects.

ΔD +
p 93(t) courtesy Anthony Blee Consultancy, photo: Henk Snoek, © Anthony Blee; Consultancy successor to Sir Basil Spence Partnership; pp 96–97 © Charles Jencks; pp 100–105 images courtesy Peter Murray; pp 106–109; p 112 courtesy Anthony Blee Consultancy, photo: Henk Snoek, © Anthony Blee; Consultancy successor to Sir Basil Spence Partnership.

Cover
Photographs © Helmut Dippold; and courtesy Van Berkel and Bos, © Christian Richters.

Subscription Offices UK
John Wiley & Sons Ltd.
Journals Administration Department
1 Oaklands Way, Bognor Regis
West Sussex, PO22 9SA
T: +44 (0)1243 843272
F: +44 (0)1243 843232
E: cs-journals@wiley.co.uk

Subscription Offices USA and Canada
John Wiley & Sons Ltd.
Journals Administration Department
605 Third Avenue
New York, NY 10158
T: +1 212 850 6645
F: +1 212 850 6021
E: subinfo@wiley.com

Annual Subscription Rates 2000
Institutional Rate: UK £135
Personal Rate: UK £90
Student Rate: UK £60
Institutional Rate: US $225
Personal Rate: US $145
Student Rate: US $105

ΔD is published bi-monthly.
Prices are for six issues and include postage and handling charges. Periodicals postage paid at Jamaica, NY 11431. Air freight and mailing in the USA by Publications Expediting Services Inc, 200 Meacham Avenue, Eimont, NY 11003

Single Issues UK: £19.99
Single Issues outside UK: US $32.50
Order two or more titles and postage is free. For orders of one title ad £2.00/US $5.00. To receive order by air please add £5.50/US $10.00

Postmaster
Send address changes to ΔD c/o Expediting Services Inc, 200 Meacham Avenue, Long Island, NY 11003

Printed in Italy. All prices are subject to change without notice.
[ISSN: 0003-8504]

The Transformable House
Guest Editors Jonathan Bell + Sally Godwin

 Architectural Design +

For architects, the allure of transformable architecture lies at least partly in the impulse to question and stretch the conventional and the given. In modern domestic architecture, this may mean experimentation with anything from standard floor plans, partitioning and walls to the perception of home itself. Rooted in the modernist's advocacy of the open floor plan, the transformable also, somewhat paradoxically, runs counter to the Modern Movement's idea of fixed architectures in which the architect is king, dictating his/her clients' environment. Never still, transformation is an inevitable condition of building over time as needs and occupiers change. It is only in recent years, however, that it has become a design prerequisite or practical consideration for present clients as the intensification of social and urban change has meant that they have greater and overlapping demands on their more minimal dwelling spaces.

This issue of Δ grew somewhat organically out of an article that Jonathan Bell wrote for *Aspects of Minimal Architecture II* (Δ, no 5/6, 1999) on the work of Mark Guard Architects. Rather than highlighting Guard's association with Minimalism, Bell pointed out that the most interesting aspect of his work was the way he was setting out to develop living spaces with a 'variable function' that adapt to 'the transient and changeable nature' of contemporary urban life. Bell had unwittingly, but no less astutely, opened our eyes at Δ to the potential of an entire issue given over to a quest for domestic flexibility.

With this title of Δ, Jonathan Bell and Sally Godwin have succeeded in delivering an issue that is entirely catholic not only in the types of architecture it includes but also in its approach to transformability. The choice of projects featured in the latter part of the issue range from the futuristic houses of Jestico & Whiles and MIT, to the finely crafted luxury of Lazzarini Pickering, to Softroom's fantasies and the more grounded solutions of Cartwright Pickard and Richard Murphy. In the opening essays, the historical period and subject changes with each authors' text, but also what it means to be transformable. Starting with Catherine Croft's description of the flexible partitions in that modern icon the Schröder House, the focus shifts to Dennis Sharp's investigation of Buckminster Fuller's unorthodox Dymaxion House designs. In his piece on the staircase in Chamberlin, Powell and Bon's Golden Lane Estate, Iain Borden brings the experiential to the fore. In contrast Glendinning and Muthesius give a more concrete account of transformation in postwar social housing. James Gallie's article on architecture for the homeless represents a whole new take on the subject – taking it to the base line – applying the notion of transformation and user participation to the most essential of shelters. If not transforming, the wide-ranging scope of this issue of Δ should at least press at received definitions of transformable architecture.

Jonathan Bell

Introduction

Right
Figure 1: Aerial view of the ground floor of the HangerHouse. Designed by Katy Ghahremani and Michael Kohn for the HangerHouse Company, the house takes the shape of the pitched-roof suburban villa, yet plays dramatically with structure and form.
The technology-filled concept house was exhibited at the 2000 Ideal Home Show.

This issue of *Architectural Design*, entitled 'The Transformable House', embraces a broad sweep of architectural history and practice. In this context, 'transformable' means many things – the integration of technology into the home, the use of modular systems to facilitate construction and planning, or the development of complex devices for modifying and customising architectural space on a day-to-day basis.

In the twentieth century, freed from classical strictures, modernists rapidly imprisoned themselves in the orthodoxy of the grid – the very grid that had been heralded as a passage to freedom, a break from the facade's slavish adherence to internal plan and decorative embellishment. However, while modern design centred on the reductivism inherent in the dictum 'form follows function', others saw in architecture the power to revolutionise social conventions through the abolition of the rigid floor plan that had dictated the separation and fragmentation of the domestic sphere. But while open-plan living may have become an integral component of modernism, its legacy is not nearly as pronounced as the other modernist conventions governing ornament, materials and form.

The 'house', a basic, freestanding unit drawing on centuries of tradition, has remained unchallenged as the most aspirational mode of living for the vast majority of the population. It is the house – the last bastion of the tyrannical patron and egotistical architect (or vice versa) – that has shaped our perception of the past century's defining architectural moments. Often exclusive, more likely divisive far beyond the modern movement's original social remit, the single, one-off house has acted as laboratory, test tube and Petri dish of new forms, technologies and living patterns.

But the century of socially progressive modernism and its talk of unity became the century of family diaspora, a fact that has shaped not only society, but also the built environment. Traditional notions of the family unit are being exploded as it fractures into small groupings, dispersed amongst the urban landscape. More young people share accommodation, the elderly are getting older, multiple marriages and extended families are on the increase. Where does this leave the conventional house? During their lifetime, those prototypes for suburban living, the terraced and the semidetached house, have been fêted as exemplary, condemned as inhumane, slavishly or inaccurately imitated and all the while adapted, extended and developed.

Arguably, there is no such thing as conventional housing, but the property market's innate conservatism discourages architectural experimentation and innovation. The converted terrace has become an icon – almost a cliché – of late twentieth-century British modernism. Strait-laced by a reactionary and inflexible planning system, innovation takes place from within, a hidden transformation that strives to re-create historical interiors through a modern idiom.

Below
Figure 2: Artist Katherina Heilein's *'Sunbathing Zone'* is a light-hearted look at the reuse of existing buildings. This alternative perspective on the archetypal New York water tank blurs the distinction between luxurious penthouse and strict utility.

As a result, we have become slavish adherents to interior design, hooked on DIY TV shows, our habits fed by anonymous warehouses stacked to the rafters with the raw materials with which to transform our daily lives. For millions, this is transformable architecture: the chance to alter one's environment depending on one's mood, one's taste, one's life style.

This issue of *Architectural Design* is not about those transformations. Nor does it aim to be a historical overview or a comprehensive survey. Instead, it draws inspiration from a wide variety of sources – historical, contemporary, built and unbuilt – in an attempt to identify a particular approach to architecture, and to trace the origins of the desire to alter our domestic environment.

The 1924 Schröder House, Gerrit Rietveld's archetypal kinetic 'transformable' dwelling, is frequently cited as one of the century's most iconic buildings. The extremely precise nature of Rietveld's brief is almost oxymoronic in terms of transformability. Was it intended as an important prototype of the transformable house, or a one-off experiment that he conspicuously failed to develop? Catherine Croft examines the practicality of the house through contemporary eyes, and reviews its status as an icon.

The interwar years, a period of high experimentation served as the crucible of modernism. Hans Scharoun, with his transportable wooden house of 1927 and 'growing house' of 1932, also explored adaptability, focusing on the use of wood as a material with an 'ability to permit a shifting, displacing and re-forming [plan]'.[1] The war in Europe halted avant-garde architectural development, and the urgency of postwar reconstruction focused on speed rather than innovation, shifting the emphasis to production. In interwar America, Richard Buckminster Fuller made public the Dymaxion House, a prototypical high-tech dwelling that would become the darling of the 1960s technologists. Dennis Sharp revisits the Dymaxion's genesis and explores its links with mass production.

Today, the concept of a flat-pack, flexibly planned house that can accommodate a number of configurations and environments is more commonplace, even outside of the ready-made trailer homes produced in their thousands for the American market. Philippe Starck has toyed with prefabricated housing, as has retail giant IKEA and even *Wallpaper** magazine, whose Wallpaper* House by Swedish architect Thomas Sandell was 'designed so that it could be set up on a beach in New South Wales, in a forest in Finland or nestled in a Chicago suburb'. The genesis of the suburban, and urban, house – transformability within a plan, transformability within a type and transformability within a use – forms the basis of several of the projects described, most notably the work of Mark Guard, Steven Holl, Stephen Varady and Lazzarini Pickering.

The material concerns that underlie Buckminster Fuller and Scharoun's work are also considered in James Gallie's essay on the architecture of disaster areas. The vast upheavals in the former Eastern Europe blighted the 1990s with a constant backdrop of violent ethnic tensions, resulting in population displacements on a scale not seen since the Second World War. Gallie examines the ongoing role of the 'instant architecture' proposed for disaster areas, a concern of the Archigram team and the early advocates of high tech, but a subject that has eluded widespread practical application. From the paper-tube housing of Shigeru Ban, to Yona Friedman's space-frame instant towns, Gallie calls for a greater understanding of the nature of such 'instant transformations'.

Ghahremani and Michael Kohn (figure 1), is a light-hearted take on portability, tying in transformation to life style and technology, and fully supported by product sponsorship and the now ubiquitous website. On the other side of the Atlantic, MIT's revolutionary House_n concept aims to provide an 'intelligent' house, interpreting its occupants' moods and demands through the total integration of sensors and new materials, creating 'strategies to allow people to develop architectural environments tailored to their specific lifestyles and budgets'.[2] 'Residential architecture, its embedded technologies and the process of creating it, are at least twenty years behind other industries', the MIT team claims. It is in the shiny surfaces of these future homes, so gleaming-new and button-filled, that we see reflections of our hopes and fears – where technology might take us, and what we will gain, or lose, in the process.

Today, house building can be broken down and reinvented by a method not normally associated with the construction industry: the transformation of building technology through the reassessment of the physical nature of construction.

Worlds away, the post-war suburbs of Levittown and Eichler's democratic modernism for the masses demonstrated a different kind of desire for transformation: the urge to control the social sphere, creating an instant and stable microcosm of society. The modern, model house, the integral generator of this societal transformation, never came to fruition – remaining a mere sprinkling of the unusual and the perverse amongst the serried ranks of semis. In early twentieth century Britain, these speculative suburbs fanned out from London's arterial roads like a spray of blood, decried by modernists, condemned by town planners, yet eagerly occupied by the public. Suddenly, all private housing was seemingly built on a similar plan, offering little or no flexibility when it came to choosing a home. It was only 'the house of the future', suburbia's mythical and long-overdue saviour, that toyed with transformability.

1999's Concept House competition was won by Pierre d'Avoine's Slim House, an adaptation of terraced housing for contemporary living. This year's winner, the HangerHouse by Katy

Iain Borden's lyrical and personal evocation of London's Golden Lane Estate, 'Stairway: Transforming Architecture in the Golden Lane', represents the other side of the coin, revealing how 'interpretations of sounds through walls, and the rhythms of life' can transform each apartment-dweller's perception of their space. By focusing on the unpredictable interaction of residents, equations are revealed that cannot possibly be foreseen by the architect. Borden's study of the staircases in Chamberlin Powell and Bon's award-winning scheme highlights the other realm of transformation – that which occurs after the space has been completed – transformation of the dynamic of daily routine through the architectural detail of integral components.

An overview of postwar British social housing by Stefan Muthesius and Miles Glendinning assesses the influences of modernist thought and theory on the planning of social housing, and charts the evolution of the high-rise. As they reveal, the emphasis in social housing was placed not on "loose-fit" dwellings that could be customised, but a range of finely differentiated types, which exactly fitted the needs of various household categories'.

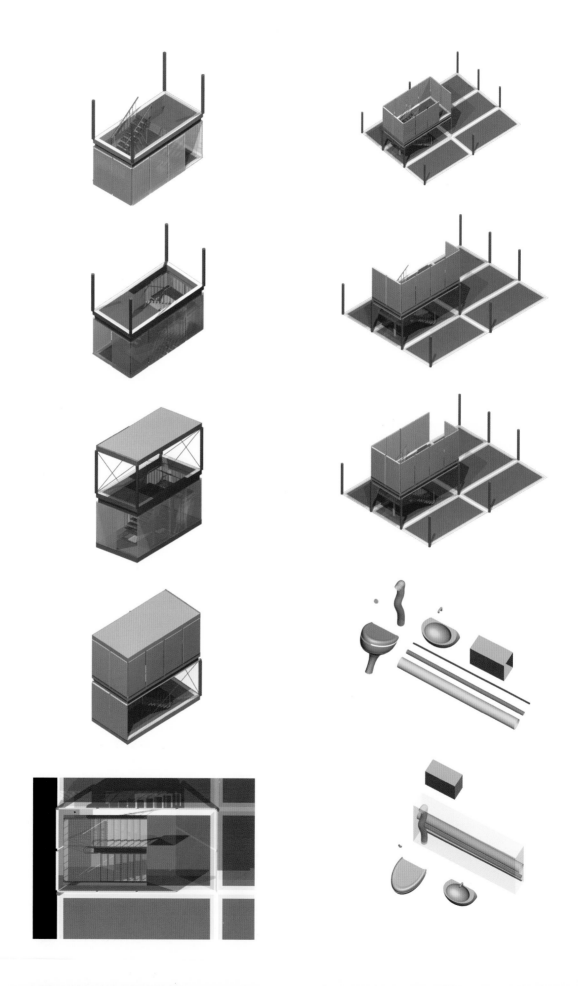

Right
Figure 3: b consultants, a
multidisciplinary group of
architects and engineers,
explored the use of a simple
modular building method,
colour-coding components
to aid construction and
reducing the home to a
series of Lego-like modules.

In contrast to this empirical study of floor plans and high-rises, fine art practitioners are using elements of architecture to explore our seemingly static relationship with the built environment, transforming and developing that which we know into that which we do not. Artists like David Thorpe, Langlands and Bell, Diller and Scofidio and Katherina Heilein (figure 2) displace us within architectural scenarios, melding the familiar and the uncertain. Catherine Wood's analysis of Thorpe's collages reveals the high-rise as a dark, brooding mass, creating strange beauty from a mundane reality.

Contemporary practice offers increasing examples of approaches to modular and prefabricated construction. Today, house building can be broken down and reinvented by a method not normally associated with the construction industry: the transformation of building technology through the reassessment of the physical nature of construction. Cartwright Pickard's, Murray Grove Housing scheme for the progressive Peabody Trust demonstrates a fundamentally modernist approach, using modular systems and extensive prefabrication. Elsewhere, the technologists b consultants, have elaborated on the functional, transportable unit with their steel, flat-pack building kit (figure 3), while architects Cottrell and Vermeulen have worked closely with Portakabin to create a classroom module, addressing the lack of appeal of this archetypal 'plug-in' building solution.

Is transformation achievable in the context of listed and historic buildings? Several of the featured projects demonstrate interventions into historic, often listed, interiors. Transformation can be gradual or instant, and the architect's approach to historical spaces remains a contentious aspect of modernism's relationship with the built environment. Carlo Scarpa, one of the most celebrated advocates of confronting past styles with new, refused to compromise his contemporary vision, yet retained a sensitive relationship with the existing building. Richard Murphy Architects strive for a similar accommodation. The Scottish practice, perhaps blessed with a more fundamentally identifiable vernacular than their cross-border counterparts, have specialised in expanding and intervening into old spaces, drawing elements of the existing into undeniably modernist schemes.

But we are all transformable now. Practitioners of plastic surgery, such as the high-profile Transform Medical Group, offer instant gratification and freedom from the burden of what we have, or haven't got. Simultaneously, scientists strive to map the human genome, decoding the vast array of genetic switches that determine our destiny, even perhaps our predilections and weaknesses. In August 1998, Professor Kevin Warwick, a researcher at the University of Reading, surgically implanted a silicon chip into his arm. 'What happens when humans merge with machines?', he asked, speculating that 'maybe the machines will then become more important to us than another human life'.[3] Heaven forbid that an architect should stray into this brave new world. But as we become increasingly digital, and the wires to our clunky, analogue selves melt away, technology's potential for transformation offers possibilities too tempting to deny for ever. During the 1990s, the increasing use of technology, and the effect this has had on architectural practice, has reopened this debate. In the past five years, hitherto undreamed of computing power has become available to the private practitioner, allowing complex theoretical approaches to be supported by the in-depth analysis of data, including movement, volume and energy use. Technology, however, is never enough.

Transformability might transcend convention – rejecting traditional life-style patterns and living arrangements in favour of a fluidity that welcomes and embraces change and difference – but innovation and the avant-garde rarely impact on our daily lives. Architecture has been lauded throughout the ages as the mother of all arts, mythologised by its practitioners and elevated through the use of complex language, deliberate obscurity and a set of almost runic symbols. It is little wonder that the concept still holds so much negative resonance for the lay person. The projects featured here span nearly 80 years, a period of immense social and technological upheaval. Over this period, architecture's integration of technology has been little more than superficial, a salve that acts as social conscience and universal solution. However, new firms are creating new modes of practice. The experiential architecture of Van Berkel and Bos, for example, shuns the 'quick fix' of technology, drawing its kinetic forms from the organic processes of everyday life. With its writhing, complex plan, their Möbius House is a reminder that transformability is all around us, at all times.

This issue of *Architectural Design* examines how architects choose to interpret and develop transformability in a re-evaluation of how we choose to live. It aims to collate the disparate threads of many long-standing architectural elements in order to bring together the aspects of design that acknowledge the potential of an open, kinetic, fluid and above all, transformable, architecture. ⟁

Notes
1. Hans Scharoun, quoted in J Christian Bürkle, *Hans Scharoun*, Artemis (Zurich), 1993, p 60.
2. Kent Larson, 'House_n: The MIT Home of the Future', paper published at http://architecture.mit.edu/~kll /body4.html.
3. Professor Kevin Warwick, 'Cyborg 1.0', *Wired Magazine*, February 2000, p 151.

Movement and Myth:
the Schröder House and Transformable Living

The Schröder House in Utrecht, designed by Gerrit
Rietveld in 1924 for his lover, Truus Schröder, and
her family is the most conspicuous modern icon of
transformable living. The inventiveness of its interiors,
which feature pioneering flexible sliding screens
and partitions, is matched by its bold aesthetic,
which adopts the strong colours and geometry of the
De Stijl movement. Here, Catherine Croft examines
its transformability and the myths that surround it.

Examining the historical origins of transformable space is a complex process. Buildings have always been required to adapt in response to a variety of changing circumstances, the most obvious being extremes of climate and expanding or contracting family size. The more interesting question is when flexibility became a generator of form, and whether it can be used to make us think differently about how we live and the choices we make.

We can trace the concept of 'transformation' to our earliest experiences – the moment when Cinderella's carriage is conjured out of a pumpkin, the wardrobe through which we are transported into a miraculous new world, or Dr Who and his Tardis. Transformation can be magical, inexplicable, an act of wish fulfilment; the most successful examples of flexible buildings share a fascination with the process of transformation and above all, a sense of wonder.

The most obvious place to start is Gerrit Rietveld's Schröder House, completed in 1924, whose upper floor is designed so that it can be completely reconfigured each day – a true

came to commission Rietveld in 1924, her circumstances were rather different from those of the mother with a small baby whose room had inspired her. In 1911, she had married Frits Schröder, a lawyer 11 years her senior, and together they had three children, two girls and a boy. She left her husband on three occasions due to disagreements about how they should be brought up. When he died, she commissioned Rietveld, who had become her lover, to design a house based on her idealistic plans for communal living. Although Rietveld was not a permanent member of the household, initially returning to his own wife and children daily, he was a frequent visitor once the house was completed.

The original concept was for a conventional plan with separate bedrooms for the children, but this was overruled on the drawing board by Schröder. The daring nature of this decision comes across in her account of the moment it happened: 'So when Rietveld had made a sketch of the rooms I asked "can those walls go too?" to which he answered, " with pleasure, away with those walls!"' However, as Schröder goes on to explain, she felt that an element of compromise was necessary:

Its compact form is especially redolent of the early phase of modernism, when the private house was the primary vehicle for radical experiment.

transformable experience (the ground floor is much more conventional). Its compact form is especially redolent of the early phase of modernism, when the private house was the primary vehicle for radical experiment, before larger programmes of public housing and other public buildings were attempted on any scale. The inspiration for the Schröder House was a vicarious experience of one-room living. Truus Schröder, whose role as client is analysed by Alice T Friedman in *Women and the Making of the Modern House* recalled: There was an occasion when I'd baby-minded for a friend of mine who lived in one large empty attic room. I sat there that evening and imagined what it would be like to live somewhere like that. I think that was the beginning for me of thinking about this sort of lifestyle.[1]

To Schröder, who was comfortably wealthy, yet felt stifled by the conventions of respectable middle-class life, this Bohemian image was strongly romantic.[2] However, by the time she

I was still looking for the possibility of also dividing up that space. That could be done with sliding partitions. I think that was an idea of Rietveld's though he found it a shame. He did it though he thought it was a pity. Personally, I'm eternally thankful that it was done.

Schröder recalled that: Rietveld always regretted [the partitions], primarily I think because the space upstairs became considerably more complicated with the placing of partitions. You see it was like having your cake and eating it: yes and no. And Rietveld would have preferred: it's either like this or like that.

Rietveld's own home, which predated the Schröder House, also strove to undermine the status quo of the fixed floor plan. As well as there being one large living area, the children's rooms were partitioned off by little more than curtains, an arrangement that Schröder 'didn't find attractive, nor did I think it would be very nice for the children'.

Central to any analysis of the Schröder House is the nature of public/private space. Surveying the house in plan, the overall layout of the first floor is clear whether the partitions are open or closed. However, for the user, the realms created by the partitions must have been clearly delineated as private. This use of space is closer to the Arts and Crafts creation of spaces within spaces: the fireside alcove, the projecting oriel at Philip Webb's Red House (1859) encouraging separate activities within a companionable larger volume (although perhaps relegating female activity to marginal zones).

Ironically, however, by rejecting any clearly defined hierarchical space, the Schröder House becomes not more egalitarian but more dictatorial. For example, any conventional notions of privacy would have been dispensed with – one would actually have to make a bathroom by pulling out walls around the bath, the antithesis of a relaxing experience. The Schröder House's mythology might place an emphasis on a pioneering form of modern free living, but the reality is about control, not freedom. It could even be said to resemble life in prison, with its proscribed actions at proscribed

times. The partitions, which are drawn at night to separate off the four corners of the space, providing separate sleeping areas for the children, do not make sense unless all are closed or all open. There is thus no scope for different time schedules – in contemporary terms, for a stroppy teenager to stay in bed until noon, or to leave filthy underwear strewn across the floor. This physical compression of family life must have placed strains on even the most unconventional set-up. Ultimately, Schröder craved greater privacy:

Truus had helped shape those spaces to suit her desires and needs but she ended up feeling enslaved by the house's fame. In 1935 she even decided to have a new, private room built. That is when the room on the roof appeared.[3]

Today, the Schröder House is no longer a home, but has been restored as a modern architectural icon, an unusual house museum. The highlight of a visit is the moment of transformation, but, even allowing for the building's age, this is ultimately a disappointment. It is hardly a 'moment' – despite Rietveld's training as a cabinet-maker, the partitions do not slide smoothly and cleanly into place; their progress in the switch from

The Rietveld-Schröder House

Hubert-Jan Henket, Chairman of the Rietveld-Schröder House Foundation, explains how Truus Schröder oversaw the evolution of her house into a museum before her death in 1984.

night to day mode is cumbersome and slow. The mechanism is curiously unsophisticated and crude – appearing to modern eyes, familiar with perfectly milled stainless steel and sparkling glass junctions, as a kind of ad hoc DIY aesthetic rather than an industrial one. The partitions are poorly fitting and do not function as walls that provide acoustic separation, or on which objects can be hung. Despite Schröder's disparagement of Rietveld's own home, they have little more presence than curtains. Even if the building is to be regarded merely as a prototype for a more sophisticated machine-made, mass-produced future, it is still unsettling. The partitions seem little more than a potentially disruptive, even traumatic, ritual at the heart of family life.

Schröder's contemporaries were more impressed by the bold use of colour, sadly lost to us in the black and white photographs that record the house's original form. The elements of De Stijl – the unconventional elevations at the end of a conventional Utrecht street – were more controversial than the interior arrangements.

However, from the beginning, reservations were raised about practicality. In 1925, JG Wattjes wrote:

> By rejecting the normal method of subdividing space – with fixed walls – and choosing a system of sliding partitions, an extremely flexible arrangement of the interior is achieved ... the intentions behind this 'machine for living in' is not that now and again you can change the arrangement of the interior, it is that each day you can alter it several times, as often as changing needs require. The question is, will such extreme flexibility in fact prove convenient in the long run? I very much doubt it.[4]

The house represents a form of intellectual alienation, from both conventional society and from conventional family arrangements.

More than any of the other buildings that make up the established modernist canon – The Villa Savoye, the Barcelona Pavilion, et al – the Schröder House combines a sense of pioneering architectural invention with close allegiance to a contemporary art movement; it is both

If you sit here you get a wonderful view of the blossoming apple tree. It was Riet's favourite spot, particularly with the windows open, because then the relationship between the nature outside and the culture inside is at its most.[1]

Truus Schröder, Gerrit Rietveld's client, collaborator and lover, talked with great warmth and enthusiasm about her beloved home, the most revolutionary house of the twentieth century, in which she lived from 1924 until 1984. Whenever the owner of a house designed specifically for them dies, the question is raised as to how to secure the authenticity of their environment for future generations without damaging its poetry.

Truus Schröder was 35 and a mother of three when her husband died in 1923. Since remaining in their large house at the Biltstraat in Utrecht was impossible, she asked Rietveld to design her a new home. Rietveld was the logical choice: he had converted the Biltstraat house a few years before, and client and architect turned out to be brothers in arms in their search for a modern way of living. Schröder wanted a small, efficient house that would not dictate a special life style. She sought sobriety and ultimate freedom of use, so that she could be independent. Greatly

intrigued by these requirements, within a matter of weeks Rietveld freed himself from more conventional solutions and presented his transformable proposal to his client. Four vertical and two horizontal planes framed the space, offering both openness and protection in a wide scale of variations.[2] The living area was situated on the first floor because Schröder wanted to live as close as possible to the sun, rain, wind and daylight. To allow this living area to be either one large space or subdivided into living room, bathroom and three bedrooms, Rietveld developed a system of movable partitions, which gives the interior its great a 'machine for living in' and an aesthetically composed work of the Dutch De Stijl movement. For many years, it was this relationship that formed the basis of critical appraisal, but the extent to which Rietveld himself saw the sliding screens and partitioning as ground breaking – something likely to have a lasting influence rather than being a highly idiosyncratic response to an individual client – is questionable.

In the recent architectural history *Mart Stam's Trousers*, an analysis of the origins of so-called Dutch Moral Modernism, Ed Taverne casts doubt on the house's reputation:

I think that Rietveld – partly under the influence of the success of his house ... began to regard his creation, in retrospect, as a protomodel for high-quality and liberated living, and as an exemplary house that, partly to the utilitarian machinery, was designed as a social therapeutic *Gesamtkunstwerk*.[5]

The insinuation that the innovative reputation of the Schröder House owes a great deal to hindsight and a revisionist attitude towards the aims of the project, is instructive. Historian Marijke Kuper agrees that the house was arranged in such a way that one had to be aware of each action, whether it was taking a bath, eating or sleeping. That meant that one had to work on it, had to do something for it: creating the bathroom and the bedroom by pushing aside walls, constructing the sofa bed, unfolding the table ... in this house, the concepts of comfort and indolence, activity and passivity, awareness and automatism were polarised to an extreme degree.[6]

Whether this was a conscious desire of the client, or merely a by-product, is debatable. But the fact that these questions are only now being asked is testament to the house's enduring aura.

Is transformability truly achievable? Countless subsequent projects have attempted to reconcile the problems of architectural permanence with the flexibility that is increasingly required in family life. Wattjes's criticism of the Schröder House highlights one way in which so called 'transformable' buildings can be

sense of dynamism. With its many clever details, the house was both a fascinating spatial experience and a pleasant and easily habitable dwelling.

Securing the specific qualities of the Schröder House for the enjoyment of future generations was in many respects relatively easy. Schröder realised in the 1950s that when Rietveld died the importance of his contribution to architecture would be considerably underestimated if his most significant work were to disappear. In 1961, Rietveld died in the house at the age of 76. Nine years later, Schröder set up the Rietveld-Schröder House Foundation, which was made responsible for safeguarding all of Rietveld's work – including an enormous archive that Schröder had acquired over the years – and for promoting interest in his ideas and work.

After Schröder's death in 1984, both the interior and the exterior of the house were extensively restored by the architect Bortus Mulder. Mulder had been an assistant in Rietveld's office and had carried out several restorations on the house when Schröder was still alive. The foundation subsequently asked him to look after the technical condition of the house on a permanent basis. In 1985, the foundation passed the responsibility of the

Notes
1. Truus Schröder quoted in Bortus Mulder and Ida van Ziji, *Rietveld Schröderhuis*, V & K Publishing, 1997.
2. See Bortus Mulder, Gerrit *Thomas Rietveld, leven, denken, werken*, SUN, Nijmegen, 1994.
3. The curator of the Rietveld archive is Ida van Ziji. It is advisable to book tours in advance by phoning the Centraal Museum, Utrecht, The Netherlands, tel: 030-236 2362 or fax: 030-233-2006.

management of the house to the Centraal Museum in Utrecht, which opened the building to the public. The Centraal Museum also keeps the Rietveld-Schröder archives, and a wing of the museum is dedicated to Rietveld's furniture, models and drawings. The Schröder House is one of the museum's top exhibits, attracting 10,000–15,000 visitors from over 50 different countries every year, even though it is a half-hour walk from the museum.

Visitors are taken through the house in groups of 12 by specially trained guides, who speak at least four languages.[3] Before the tour, a video about Rietveld's work is shown in the information centre, located in a rented apartment on the ground floor of the house next door. The maintenance costs of the house are paid for from the interest from a fund donated by the insurance company AMEV, and the annual deficit of around $110,000 is picked up by the Centraal Museum, itself owned by the Utrecht municipality. Of course, the decision to keep the house in a more or less authentic state for eternity is contrary to the natural cycle of birth, usage and degradation and, as a result, the atmosphere is now different from the time when Schröder and Rietveld lived there. But while the cost of maintaining the house is high, it is universally considered to be well worth the effort and expense. After a long period in which the unique qualities of this very special house could be enjoyed only by a happy few, it can at last be experienced by everyone. ◭

Notes
1. Alice Friedman, *Women and the Making of the Modern House: a Social and Architectural History*, Abrams, New York, 1998. The Schröder House is discussed with Maristella Casciato in *Family Matters: The Schröder House* by Gerrit Rietveld and Truus Schröder', pp 64–91. All Schröder's quotations regarding the construction of the house are taken from this source.
2. The attic metaphor and its connotations of freedom and rebelliousness must have gained strength when it became clear that the way to get around local building regulations was to designate the first floor of the Schröder House an 'attic'.
3. *Domus*, September 1987.
4. JG Wattjes, *Stories from behind the Scenes of Dutch Moral Modernism*, Crimson (with Michael Speaks and Gerard Hadders), Mart Stam's Trousers, 010 Publishers, Rotterdam, 1999.
5. Ed Taverne, '*The only truly canonical building in Northern Europe*', Crimson (with Michael Speaks and Gerard Hadders), Mart Stam's Trousers, 010 Publishers, Rotterdam, 2000, p 106.
6. Quoted in the above.
7. Miriam Howitt, *One Room Living*, Design Council, 1972.

categorised – Rietveld's project is unusually ambitious in that it is intended for daily (or even more frequent) transformation. Later buildings have rarely sought to emulate this flexibility, especially not when they are designed to serve more than a single occupant. More satisfactory projects have arisen from buildings that transform in response to climatic changes, or can be altered at widespread intervals to accommodate a growing family or other gradually shifting circumstances.

Another project that acknowledges the need of the occupier to control the nature of the space is Haworth Tompkins' Royal Court Theatre in London. The theatre has a long and specific tradition of transformation, from complex wooden scenery slots and trapdoors, to other ingenious bits of stage machinery, manipulated to create the magical illusion of 'transformation scenes', as day turns to night, or Cinderella becomes a princess. Early twentieth-century mechanical inventiveness focused on the auditorium, with movable towers of seating on air castors, ingenious lifts and folding elements that allowed a space to be reconfigured from flat-floored hall to traditional proscenium arch theatre, to theatre-in-the-round. Few of these proved lastingly successful, however, failing either spatially in one or sometimes all formats,

and proving slow and expensive to operate. The Royal Court's transformation is hidden in its core: the dressing rooms have elaborate external screening shutters in perforated Cor-ten steel. The shutters can be operated from within each dressing room and are explicitly chunky, as are the operating levers and wheels, celebrating the process of transformation and the knowledge that the actor is exercising control. He or she can draw back the screens to look out over a public yard or withdraw behind a physically robust shuttered barrier which has echoes of Islamic balcony screens and their connotations of protective privacy. A theatrical analogy is created by allowing the actors to generate private space before the public appearance, or letting them control their gradual 'unveiling' through the use of the steel shutters.

I remember as a child repeatedly renewing a DIY book at the library. *One Room Living*,[7] riding on the bedsit boom of the 1970s, was a riot of space-saving ideas: bunk beds on top of fold-out kitchens, ingenious stacking, concertina-style storage units and other tips for the tightly packed urbanist who needed to utilise every inch of space. Wipe-down surfaces and knock-down fittings could transform life. Alas, not mine. I longed to carve up my bedroom, or better still, escape spacious suburbia for a canal boat, a camper van or at the very least, a tent. However, I was thwarted by a moratorium on power tools and a claustrophobic mother. My godfather, a D'Oyly Carte fanatic, once took us to see a little-known Gilbert and Sullivan opera, *Cox and Box*, which pleased me further with its spatial efficiency. In an early precursor to hot-desking, Mr Cox and Mr Box worked opposite shifts and unknowingly rented out the same room. In those days, I would have loved the ingenuity and economy of the Schröder House, but by the time I got to see it, it horrified me. It should be acknowledged, however, that it functions perfectly as an iconic building, a symbol both of modernist living and a pioneering art movement. ⊅

Buckminster Fuller's
Mechanical Houses:

Maximum Deployment
in a Dymaxion World

If transformability was nurtured by the International
Movement's insistence on the free plan, it was invigorated
by the inventions of the wholly idiosyncratic American
individualist Richard Buckminster Fuller. Dennis Sharp
describes how Fuller's 1927 designs for the Dymaxion
House — a neologism signifying 'dynamism plus efficiency'
— based on techniques drawn from the aircraft and
vehicle industries, became a universal prototype for
low-cost mass production.

For one inventor at least, 1927 was a good year. In his autobiography, Richard Buckminster Fuller commented that it was in this year that 'I learned to see myself'.[1] Referring to what he called his 'personal scientific journey' in the years from 1917, during which he was known as 'Guinea Pig B' (B for Bucky), he wrote:

It persuaded me ten years later to start my life as nearly "anew" as it is humanely possible to do'. The hero of Bucky's self-proclaimed 'second life' after 1927 was Robin Hood: 'I took away Robin Hood's longbow, staff and checkbook and gave him scientific textbooks ... and industrialisation's network of tooling. I made him substitute new inanimate forms for animate reforms.

Buckminster Fuller (1895–1983) was born on 12 July in Milton, Massachusetts, USA. After a brief period at Harvard and the US Naval Academy, he served in the navy. In 1927 – aged 32 – he published his first privately printed monograph, *4-D Time Lock*, which announced his ideas for a Dymaxion world. Two years later, his Dymaxion House was on show in model form in Chicago, where it was billed as a design 'produced by factory methods on a quality production basis'.

The 4-D Dymaxion House was made public in 1928, having gone through many minor modifications. It was a design for a new way of domestic living, suggesting the mobility and speed of modern life, its temporary nature and expandability. 'Dwellings are environment-controlling machines', Bucky pronounced, just as cars were becoming miniature palaces, air-conditioned and electrified. His house for the new scientific and technological age was to be of Duralumin (a strong, low-density aluminium alloy used in aircraft), and would be a living machine based on a triangular module and suspended from a mast containing centralised services.

The tree-shaped Dymaxion House was to be applicable as a single unit or as a series set in a town, a forest, or built up as a modular high-rise fashioned on the pagoda principle. Fuller, however, claimed that it was an invention with 'purely theoretical significance'. It was no more than 'a statement of a problem ... rather than a fixed solution, an attitude of willingness to think truthfully' about housing and mass production. In fact, it was an essay in the concept of the house as a living machine, an ideal fostered by many at the time, including Le Corbusier with his *machine à habiter* and Bruno Taut with his earlier notion of a *Wohnmaschine*.

Right
Dymaxion Deployment Unit for military and civilian use, c. 1928.

The Duralumin mast supporting the house was anchored to the ground at its base. The sunken pedestal forming part of this anchorage housed the storage and septic tanks for heating fuel and for sewerage. The house was to be 40 feet high and 50 feet across, and earthquake-flood-tornado and marauder-proof. Its two bedrooms each had a bath and pneumatic beds. It was to have sealed windows and be fully air-conditioned, the walls double-lined with a vacuum-sealed space between layers. Steel tension cables hanging from the top of the mast supported tubular floor beams in compression that formed a hexagonal ring. Thin, triangular metal plates were connected to the frame and mast by tensioned wires to form a floor deck which, in order to prevent sagging, was covered with a pneumatic floor system. An independent roof hood was supported from the main mast to protect the upper deck area. It was calculated

that a house would weigh some 6,000 lb and its cost was estimated in 1928 as $3,000 delivered.

The Dymaxion House project was contemporary with the model mass-housing experiments of the European Functionalists at the Stuttgart *Weissenhofsiedlung* and other Werkbund estates that followed in Vienna and Breslau. It was, however, a completely different kind of prototype from the experimental houses of the European modernists. Its forms and spatial configuration had little to do with the development of a Functionalist aesthetic, or with the so-called International styling that was deemed to be a common characteristic of early modern movement housing. Fuller was pursuing an unrelated and completely different tack.

By 1927, Bucky's work was well ahead of the kind that was going on in Europe, or even the later architectural, industrial and social programmes for the prefabrication of mass housing in the USA. His approach at that time was much more inventive and original and, of course, because it was the result of a lifetime's

Below (main)
Geodesic Dome near Montreal, December 1950.

Below (Inset)
Standard of Living Package with Geodesic Cover, Black Mountain College, 1949.

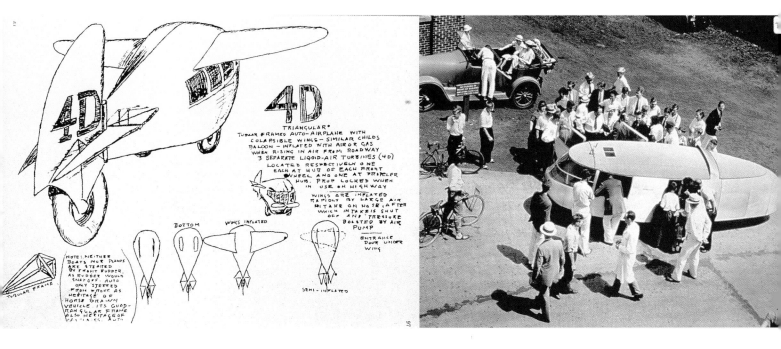

Above left
Sketch for 4D transportation, 1928. The teardrop shape of the Dymaxion car finally finds its wings.

Above right
Dymaxion Car No 1, July 1933.

philosophy, much more personal. This was a period of deployment for Bucky.

Following its publication in American architectural journals from 1928 onwards, the Dymaxion House spawned numerous inventions and innovations in the housing industry, from DIY to the mobile home and camper. As an idea, it was considered, but not used, in the USSR and Europe as well as the USA. The Dymaxion House provided fuel for a potential mass attack on the housing problems of the USA, but sadly its introduction virtually coincided with the introduction of economic restraints imposed by the Wall Street crash of 1929. This meant it had little chance of being taken up in practice at the time, and no chance of moving beyond the figurative ideas that Bucky had set out to prove in his original project models and drawings. As a concept for adaptive and extensible housing, however, it was neither overlooked nor neglected. Indeed, in an official British government survey into prefabrication undertaken in 1945 by the architect Dex Harrison on behalf of the Ministry of Works, Fuller's Dymaxion House was applauded for its didactic qualities. The report claimed that it 'merits the closest of study' precisely because it was indicative of 'potentialities not foreseen by the more orthodox systems' and its early suggestions 'for light metals and plastics and its mechanical core' were duly noted.[2]

For Fuller, the house provided the kick-start for a series of related inventions including a Dymaxion Traffic Chart (reproduced in *4-D Time*

Lock), a sheet-metal bathroom and the Dymaxion Deployment Unit, which was a four-piece, copper, prefabricated kitchen-bathroom unit that could be mounted on wheels. It could then be attached to any building and transported to another site if the occupant wished to move. However, the invention that attracted the greatest attention was undoubtedly Fuller's remarkable Dymaxion Car, a vast, teardrop-shaped three-wheeler with aerodynamic pretensions that predated Detroit's early brushes with streamlining. This amphibian aeroplane-automobile design was intended to be part of the house's standard equipment.

As Europe and the US became caught up in the Second World War, Bucky went through hard times until his skill as a cartographer brought its own rewards. In the US during these years, he gained a reputation for inventiveness largely through the design of his own house at Wichita, NY, a small dome structure that was widely publicised. It was in these lean times that he developed the most imitated form of lightweight protective cover devised by man in the last century: the geodesic dome. At the time of the anniversary of his 100th birthday in 1995, it was estimated that some 400,000 geodesic examples had been erected throughout the world. The geodesic dome, which incorporated at least some of the ideas from the earlier Dymaxion programmes, particularly in the use of mast and guys, had, literally, come home. Many habitable examples were built throughout the world. Along with his world map, the geodesic dome may have been Bucky's most popular invention, but his Dymaxion ideas and their deployment will remain his most fertile. ⌂

Notes
1. All Richard Buckminster Fuller quotations are from his autobiography *Critical Path*, Hutchinson (London), 1983 or 1981.
2. Dex Harrison, Survey of Prefabrication, Ministry of Works (London), 1945, (mimeographed) sourced from AF Bemis, *The Evolving House*, (New York), vol 3, 1936.

A major retrospective, 'Buckminster Fuller: Your Private Sky', runs at the Design Museum in London from 15 June to 15 October 2000.

Stairway:
Transforming
Architecture
in the Golden Lane

Though the openness or flexibility of a house is generally deemed to be expressed in its floor plan, the greatest transformation in conventionally planned domestic spaces occurs vertically. The staircase is the instrument of movement from the public realm of downstairs to the private domain of upstairs. Iain Borden describes how the internal staircase in his own home, in a flat in Chamberlin, Powell and Bon's 1962 Golden Lane Estate in London, transforms the architecture both experientially and visually.

The concrete interior staircase is a menace and a source of noise from my next-door neighbours.[1]

We don't think enough about staircases.
Nothing was more beautiful in old houses
than the staircases.
Nothing is uglier, more hostile, meaner,
in today's apartment buildings.
We should learn to live more on staircases.
But how?[2]

In the typical house typologies of England, the internal stairway is conventionally enclosed by walls, that is, the stairway is contained within a staircase. Hidden from view (except, of course, when one is actually ascending or descending the stairway and, even then, it is amazing how many people do not consciously look at the tricky construction they are negotiating), the stairway is treated as a distasteful device, like a dumbwaiter for the moving of dishes, a country house backstairs for the circulation of servants or, worse still, a rubbish chute down which debris periodically tumbles. Within the staircase, an even more forgotten space lurks: the under-stair cupboard, which, if one is brave enough to peer inside, one finds to be stuffed with acrid-smelling cleaning fluids, musty rain-gear and, in the most rearward and inaccessible niches, God-only-knows-what-else. Both stairway and cupboard are boxes within the staircase, into which one ventures darkly and as infrequently as possible.

A stairway with which I am intimately acquainted assumes a quite different attitude. My home is a 1950s two-floor maisonette, part of a medium-sized estate constructed on a large bomb-site for London's City Corporation and now known as the Golden Lane. The intended residents, who still form the majority of the estate's inhabitants, were local single people and couples (not large families), many of whom worked nearby at Bart's hospital and Smithfield meat market.

These residents would have been quite accustomed to the more constricted rooms and staircases of tenement flats, terraced rows and subdivided urban villas. Despite this clientele, or perhaps because of it, the architects – Joe Chamberlin, Geoffrey Powell and Christopher Bon – chose to celebrate the stairway, having it rise directly out of the living room. In order to open the space below the stairs, and in complete denial of traditional cupboard storage, there is no evident support within the room – no lower wall, no stringer between the treads, no supportive columns and no veiling screen. Instead, the treads are individually cantilevered from the side wall, projecting outwards in a heroic yet commonplace gesture. This is most apparent whenever the sun shines through the large south window at the base of the stairway, when the shadows that radiate out across the bare side wall proclaim the treads' fantastical existence free from the constraints of gravitational physics. Even the newel post (in fact a sweeping continuation of the handrail), which on first sight might appear to be providing some kind of ground-based support, passes clean through a neat circular hole in the lowermost tread. The startling simplicity of construction is underlined by the balusters, or more precisely by their fixing nuts, exposed beneath the treads, whose crude nature boldly states that what you see is indeed what you get. This stairway has no deathly, shrouding coffin.

Architectural historians will be quick to note that this stairway arrangement may well have been adapted from Le Corbusier's Unité d'Habitation in Marseilles, whose construction finished the same year, 1952, that Chamberlin, Powell & Bon won the Golden Lane competition. Others will be equally quick to point out that another entry for the Golden Lane competition, the infamous street-deck scheme by the Smithsons, has been far more influential upon subsequent architectural developments.

Yet it is not the placing of the Golden Lane stairway within the canon of modernism that gives it architectural life. More important is the way in which each stairway is integrated into the flat as a whole, for as a contemporary architectural magazine noted, the 'volume of the stair running through the two floors and the two-storey window associated with it become a visual part of the living room'.[3] How, then, does this staircase 'become a visual part of the living room'? What is this process of becoming? What is the relationship and in what way is it visual, and how is the architecture transformed as a result?

The answer lies not just in the visual or spatial analysis of the stairway, although such things do play their part, and the stairway can, of course, be seen in plan, section, elevation, photograph, direct experience and all the other ways of observing a piece of architecture. But such representations as plans and even sections do little to articulate the more dynamic aspects of architecture, particularly those involving verticality. As the German architectural theorist Paul Frankl wrote in 1914:

> To understand a secular building we must get to know it as a whole by walking through it ... The entrance, the vestibule or passage leading to courtyard or stair, the connections between several courtyards, the stairs themselves and the corridors leading away from them at each level, like the veins of our bodies – these are the pulsating arteries of a building.[4]

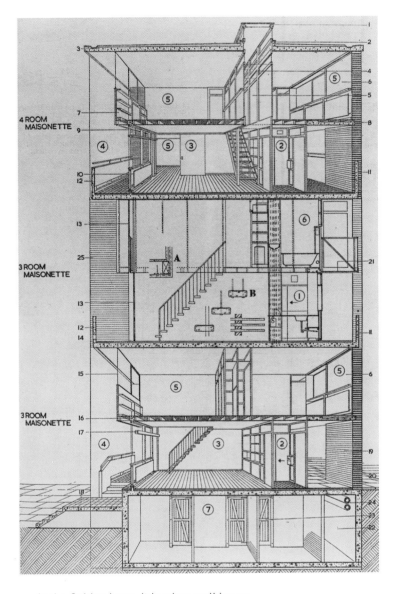

At the Golden Lane, it is when walking up and down, as one must repeatedly do during the course of daily routines, that one first encounters the unique phenomenological character of these stairs. Such a condition was recognised by the modernist British architect Berthold Lubetkin when he remarked that 'any staircase is a sort of machine to climb up or to descend, but in the best Beaux Arts interpretation it is a display, it is a dance'. Lubetkin continues, 'and it certainly enriches the conception of human surroundings and the body if architecture can bring in everyday experience a sort of ballet-like quality – semipoetic choice – in what otherwise is a purely utilitarian conception'.[5] Such a stairway is more than a conveyor belt; it is also a social stage.

While the quotidian body may be transformed into that of a dancer through the device of the stairway, so too is another transformation effected upon the stairs themselves. When experienced by the motile and rhythmic body, the treads are revealed as individual planes: each forward step is met by a corresponding, independently supported platform on which to tread and, simultaneously as the steps continue, by a connected series of such planes; the stairs are at once unique and repeated, autonomous and integrated. Ascending and descending, combining bent knees, measured steps and a cautiously balancing hand (for the Golden Lane stairway is unusually steep, a fact brought into sharp relief by the absence of solid risers), one enunciates these stairs as a sentence, a chain of moments and movements, each unique in itself yet inseparable from the others. Walking creates a unity of the stairs; hence it is the act of movement together with the architecture, and not the architecture by itself, that makes the stairway. These stairs are as pearls on a necklace, complete qua necklace only when placed against the body.

It is not, however, simply that the stairway is a production of bodily space and movement, for, as in baroque stairs, it itself is also a focus of attention,[6] an intellectual as well as material endeavour. At Golden Lane, just as walking unites the stairway and the stairway unites walking, so too does the stairway give aesthetic expression to the possibility of movement – each cantilevered tread, ever visible to the eye, suggests that walking on these treads is not only possible but probable, and hence that the floors of the flat are continually interrelated. In a further reinforcement of this view, the vertical metal balusters are, although evenly spaced horizontally, given a 1:2:1 rhythm across the series of treads. Each tread is thus expressed separately yet as part of the series, with a dynamic composition subtly transferring the eye from one to another. Through such aesthetic operations, the stairway offers the continual reminder that there are other spaces within the maisonette, and that habitation conjoins them together. The same could perhaps be said of the double-height space that sits over the stairway, for this too gives volumetric connection between floors. Yet it is only the eye and not the body that travels in this space (indeed, I have physically entered it only once, in order to complete a precarious piece of DIY).The stairway, by contrast, is the more corporeal element, encouraging the resident to pursue both mentally and physically the arch-modernist Sigfried Giedion's assertion that in order 'to grasp the true nature of space

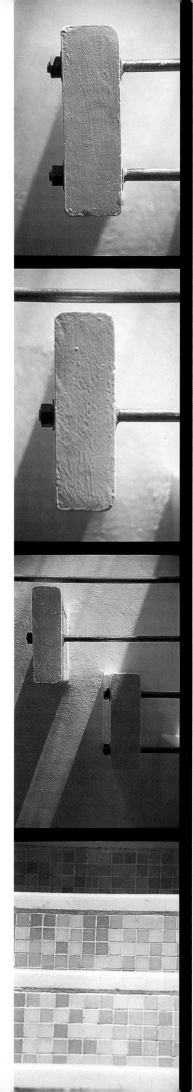

All photos are by Iain Borden.

the observer must project himself through it'.[7] Whether located in the living room or the upper landing, the visibility and detail of the stairway both promotes movement and gives expression to the possibility of that movement. Indeed, this facet of the stairway is revealed in the very naming of its parts, where the step, tread, going, flight and riser are, along with the door handle, near-unique in architecture in being not only the noun given to the element in order to identify it but also the verb used to describe the bodily encounter with that element: we step and tread on a stairway, we go along, we fly and rise up, and we handle door furniture. This very nomenclature demands that an action, and an overtly bodily action at that, be performed against the element, the essence of which ultimately lies not within the material or form of the architecture but in its reproduction within the motile body and within the expressive means (language and architectural design) by which we represent that reproduction.

After living in this flat for a while, another connection also gradually makes its presence felt. The stairs are made from hard terrazzo (although in our home they have been covered with paint and tiles) and when trod upon, each creates a distinct sound, such that every descent and ascent provides a short, repetitive melody to the life of the flat – a keyboard of everyday movements, punctuating space with its peculiar form of music. (It is perhaps no coincidence that the hi-fi in our flat is placed beneath the stairway; unconsciously, this area has been made into the sound-hearth of the home.)

Nor is it just one's own flat that is enervated so. While there are no public-stairway social condensers in the Golden Lane – those spaces beloved by the designers of social housing where residents are expected unavoidably to meet and thus forge new social relations – the internal stairways nonetheless act in their own small way within this social frame. Each cantilevered tread is balanced by its mirror-element on the other side of the party wall, creating exactly the same stairway for the flat next door. And so my paced sound-rhythms are transmitted with extraordinary efficiency through the terrazzo to my South African neighbours, just as their sounds are to me, creating a sonorous, social connection between our otherwise separate existences. After some years, I know when they sleep and when they arise, I know when they are in a hurry and when A has put on high heels, just as they must know the same kinds of detail about us.

This, perhaps, is what is so intriguing about the stairway: its continual shifting from one condition to another. What goes up must come down, what is moving is also rendered as aesthetic form, what is given is always returned. The stairway may at first seem to be a linear arrangement, but in fact it is a transformative cycle, periodically rendering architecture and everyday life into a new and delightful composition. Δ

Notes
1. Letter from Golden Lane resident of 30 years to the author, 9 July 1997.
2. Georges Perec, *Species of Spaces and Other Pieces* Penguin (London) 1997), p 38.
3. Anon, 'Flats: City of London Chamberlin, Powell and Bon', *The Architectural Review*, vol 115 no 685, June 1954, p 52.
4. Paul Frankl, *Principles of Architectural History: the Four Phases of Architectural Style, 1420–1900*, MIT (Cambridge, Mass), 1973, p 78.
5. Berthold Lubetkin, quoted in John Allan, *Berthold Lubetkin, Architecture and the Tradition of Progress*, RIBA Publications (London), 1992, p 540.
6. See Amelia Gibson, 'From the Landing to the Lobby: Stairways and Elevators, an Experiential History of Vertical Movement', Master's dissertation, The Bartlett, University College London, 1996. p 31.
7. Sigfried Giedion, *Space, Time and Architecture: the Growth of a New Tradition*, Harvard University Press (Cambridge, Mass), 1963, fourth edition, p 432.

Continuity and Change

Social Housing Types in the Postwar Reconstruction era

In the postwar period, public housing in the UK underwent a vast transformation. This did not culminate in the freeplanning of interior space, as espoused by proponents of the International Style, but, as Miles Glendinning and Stefan Muthesius explain, in a concentration on free space on the exterior of housing blocks and in the wider urban ensemble.

Introduction

This article presents an overview of the innovations in the plan types of post-1945 social housing in the UK. It is a vast subject, and this brief paper necessarily consists largely of generalised statements. We are concerned here not with a handful of avant-garde, elite modernist experiments, but with a national mass-housing programme that was overseen by large public authorities, local government politicians and administrative bureaucracies, and mostly built by private building contractors. Many innovative designers worked in these public authorities, but the overall framework of large-scale command planning ensured that their diverse experiments in the transformation of domestic house planning took a rather coarse-grained form, emphasising new types of tall blocks of flats and novel dispositions of accommodation within them. The rooms in those blocks and dwellings remained fairly compartmentalised, and there were very few attempts to provide for user customisation. Thus, far from being concerned with 'floor plans' at the micro-level, this article focuses on general types and arrangements of blocks; nor do we deal with the linked matter of the spatial and social context of the modern blocks, nor with the question of 'density'.[1]

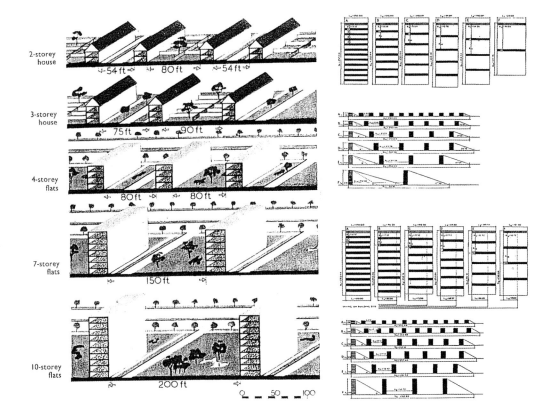

Opposite
Neave Brown, Alexandra Road, Camden, late 1960s

Top
The Zeilenbau planning concept of the 1930s and 1940s: a geometrical demonstration of the claimed advantages of high flats in maximising light and greenery. Right: Walter Gropius' analysis in *The New Architecture and the Bauhaus*, 1935. Left: a simplified version of Gropius' diagram, in EJ Carter and E Goldfinger, *The County of London Plan*, 1943.

TYPICAL 3-BEDROOM FLATS

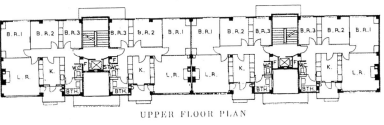

UPPER FLOOR PLAN

TYPICAL 2-BEDROOM FLATS

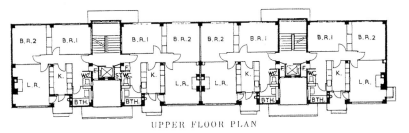

UPPER FLOOR PLAN

Bottom
2 Floor plans of a pioneering Zeilenbau project at Countess Road, Walthamstow, near London (1946 onwards, by FG Southgate): six-storey slabs with maximum light penetration from two sides and economic concentration of pipework for kitchens and bathrooms; other services are grouped separately on the ground floor. (Cement and Concrete Association, Flats at Countess Road, Walthamstow, 1949).

GROUND FLOOR PLAN

'Need/Fit' Planning:
The Propagation of modern Flats

The story of innovation in postwar house layouts is above all the story of new types of blocks, and of adjustments – rather than revolution – in the general arrangement of dwellings within them. Before the Second World War, 'council houses' in England had mostly been two-storey cottages whose plans adhered to the Parker/Unwin type of through-living room plans or the interwar 'universal plan'. In Scotland, the large and relatively undifferentiated rooms of nineteenth-century tenements had been perpetuated in a miniaturised form in interwar flats. Most postwar council housing actually remained fairly faithful to those conservative patterns, especially in Wales and Northern Ireland, and in Scottish and English rural districts, and areas with mining subsidence. What we are concerned with here, above all, is the building programmes of the cities and the new towns. In those places, there was a social hierarchy of innovation. The initial propagation of avant-garde ideas by London-based or continental critics and propagandists was followed by the working out of detailed prescriptions and type plans by the architectural and planning 'teams' and research groups of design-minded public authorities, such as the London County Council (LCC), Cumbernauld New Town Development Corporation, the Ministry of Housing and Local Government (England/Wales), or Sheffield and Coventry City Councils. Those patterns, propagated by government design manuals and the architectural press, were then routinely reproduced on a nationwide scale by the designers of other public authorities and 'package deal' private contractors.

The initial stimulus to innovation was the conviction of 1940s Modern Movement propagandists that, in order to bring light, space and greenery to the industrial cities, tall blocks of flats were necessary. In England, interwar private flats had established an association with 'luxury' amenities (including lifts and central heating) not economically available in small houses; now these 'mod cons' were to bring modern living to all classes. This advocacy went hand in hand with the evolution of new construction methods, especially using reinforced concrete. These potentially facilitated both high building and greater freedom of planning within high blocks, but that freedom was restricted in methods that relied on loadbearing walls rather than columns; significantly, full steel frames were too expensive for public housing, except in rare cases.[2]

Overall, the post-war modernists' interpretation of 'freedom' and 'flexibility' in dwelling design was orientated towards the rationalistic, scientific ethos of the age, and in particular, towards the 'need/fit' principle of social provision exactly tailored to social need, as defined by experts. The 'user' was important, but at this stage, still as a passive consumer rather than a participant. Thus, what was needed was not 'loose-fit' dwellings that could be customised, but a range of finely differentiated types that exactly fitted the needs of various household categories. This logic culminated in the LCC's 'mixed development' principle of the early 1950s, which distinguished household types within each development not only by house type but also by block type (small flats in tower blocks, larger dwellings in lower flats and cottages). The unceasing search for the optimum dwelling required far more design effort by architects and planners – but that was gladly given, as their contribution to the building of the welfare state. Key public architects and local politicians, as well as sociological researchers such as the LCC's Margaret Willis, assumed that tower blocks with modern amenities would command wide public popularity. In 1955, Lewis Womersley, Sheffield City Architect, estimated that 25-50 percent of all households would prefer to live in high flats.[3]

Slab Blocks

The innovative modernist blocks of the 1940s, 50s and 60s fell into several broad categories and phases. The first of these was the flat, sheer slab block, ranging in height from around 15 storeys to as little as three floors. This pattern had the longest pedigree in rationalised interwar Continental housing, where Walter Gropius had elaborated it into a general planning principle for residential areas – the so-called Zeilenbau principle of rigidly parallel rows of slabs, their height and orientation maximising light and space. Internally, the sheer slab block was generally associated, like nineteenth-century Scottish tenements, with shallow plans and 'through' flats, ventilated on both sides and (in its Zeilenbau form) with maximum lighting from east and west.

With its long external walls and short internal walls, the slab block became associated especially with rationalised construction methods that divided the blocks into regularly spaced compartments – for example the 'crosswall' principle, which was used for medium-rise as well as high-rise flats, or the 'box frame' or 'egg crate' method, which compartmented the block horizontally as well as vertically. Despite these restraints, there was a new freedom within each structural unit, which was exploited in the 'maisonette'. This two-storey flat type, already well known by modernists through Corbusier's immeuble-villas,

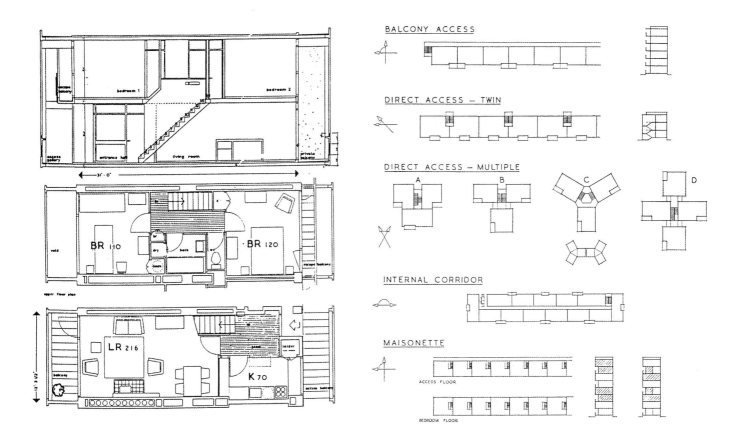

Top left
Powell and Moya, four-storey
blocks at Pimlico, London,
from 1946.

Top right
Late 1940s permutations
of access to flats and
maisonettes.

Right
Slab blocks at Powell and
Moja's Churchill Gardens,
Pimlico.

which combined elements of terraced houses in stacked form, was first used as part of four-storey blocks by Powell & Moya at Pimlico, London, from 1946. The maisonette, which was initially advocated simply as a large flat with 'the feeling of a private house', should of course be distinguished from the 'duplex' – an abortive 1940s proposal for transformable housing in the form of two-storey blocks of flats suitable for later amalgamation into houses.[4]

One of the key constraints in the planning of blocks of flats was the positioning of the access ways to the upper floors. The need to avoid punctuating crosswalls posed a problem for internal staircase/lift access in slab blocks, and access by external balcony became most popular from the 1950s. From 1951, this formula came under the influence of Le Corbusier's almost completed Unité block in Marseille. In London, the Unité's complex structure and intricate plan, combining two-storey maisonettes, flats and internal access corridors, was simplified and modified into a combination of box-frame construction and identical maisonettes. Access was still mostly by external balcony, but some slab blocks with small flats had a central internal corridor. In 1953, Leslie Martin and other LCC designers produced a new 'narrow frontage' maisonette. Only 11 feet wide, with an internal bathroom, it was used mainly in the context of 11-storey slab blocks. Although the sheer slab, from outside, seemed a fairly unified and homogeneous type, that impression was illusory, since any one of at least half a dozen major plan permutations might lie inside it.[5]

Point Blocks
During the 1950s, the dominance of the slab block was challenged by a new type, not inherited from pre-war modernism: the slender 'point block', which was hailed in 1958 by a German writer as 'the only new housing form developed since the war'. Its central principle was a stair, lift and service core, with flats arranged compactly around. The main impetus came from the Swedish punkthus type, built in the mid-1940s at Stockholm: massive blocks with internal staircases, bathrooms and kitchens. The introduction of somewhat slenderer point blocks at the LCC's Portsmouth Road estate at Roehampton in 1951 heralded the beginning of the LCC's new housing architecture. Point blocks had advantages over Zeilenbau slabs on small or hilly sites, and cast less of a shadow on the surrounding landscape, but fewer flats received the optimum amount of light.[6]

Owing to the compressed plan, point block construction was less systematised than in the case of slab blocks. Many more walls, proportionately speaking, had to be loadbearing, and crosswall planning was hardly possible. Internal layouts were more complex, as it was necessary to balance the cost advantages and arguably greater aesthetic elegance of a compact, square plan against the requirements of ventilation, lighting and fire precaution, which might be satisfied more easily with short projecting wings. Matters were made easier in London from 1954, when a new fire code required only one incombustible staircase. The sub-varieties of these two point-block-plan families were probably uncountable, but the most ubiquitous layout by the time of massed reproduction in the mid-1960s featured a central lift core and either four or six one/two-bedroom flats on each upper floor. Larger flats of three or more bedrooms, and certainly maisonettes, were more difficult to fit into the more compact setting of the point block. By the late 1950s and early 1960s, these compact blocks were reaching far greater heights – for example, 31-storey point blocks (in steel frame construction) at Red Road, Glasgow, in 1962. At the same time, the LCC and other authorities were pioneering new, denser and more massive types of tower block, some including maisonettes as well as flats.[7]

Agglomerative Blocks
The peak of the development of internal complexity in the plans of modern flats in the UK was reached in the 1960s. This complexity was associated neither with point nor slab blocks, but with a third generation of multi-storey housing – a medium-height conglomerate of different types of flats and maisonettes, reached by various kinds of access within blocks of extreme complexity of plan and section.

Two main influences contributed to this complex type. The first was the LCC's development of new slab-block types in the late 1950s and early 1960s, with much more intricate, multi-level cross sections. This 'sectional' planning was largely indebted to Le Corbusier, whose block cross-sections were compared to 'anatomical drawings' in 1964 by the Architectural Review. It meant that horizontals and verticals were no longer continuous. Within the single dwelling, the floor was not on one level, or on two floors exactly above each other, as in the case of the standard maisonette. The LCC 'scissors' type of 1962 took the idea of an indoor corridor between maisonettes from Corbusier's Unité, but complicated it further by splitting the levels of the flats (eg at Abbeyfield Road, Banner Street and Royal Victoria Yard developments).[8]

The second influence was the emergence of the 'deck access' housing type in the mid-1950s – a development of balcony access from a merely practical

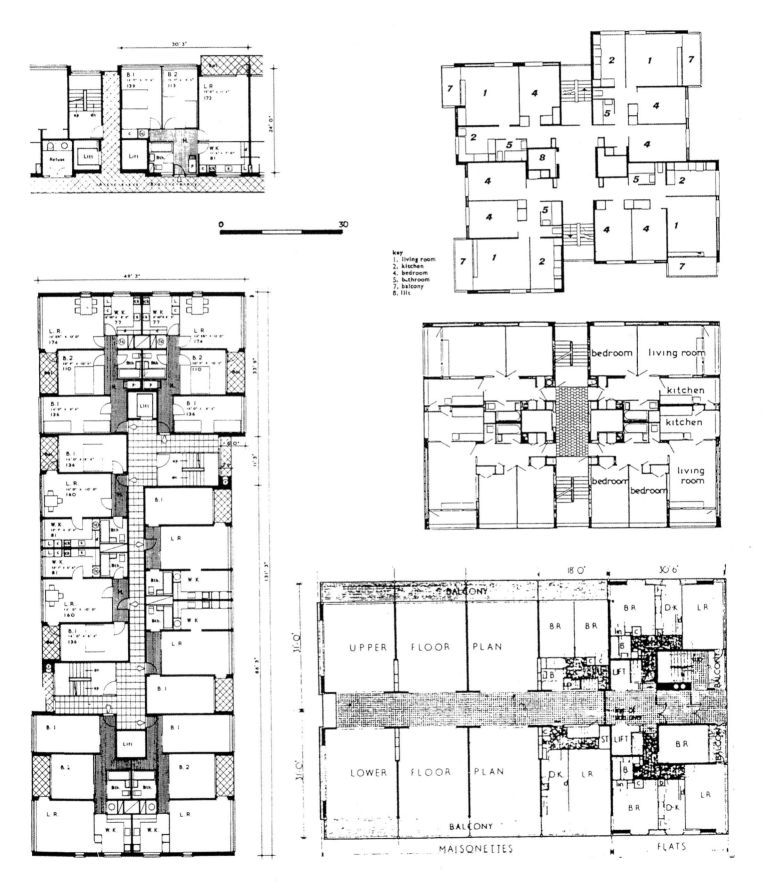

key
1. living room
2. kitchen
4. bedroom
5. bathroom
7. balcony
8. lift

UPPER FLOOR PLAN

LOWER FLOOR PLAN

MAISONETTES

FLATS

bedroom living room

kitchen

kitchen

bedroom bedroom living room

Notes
1. For more detailed references, see Miles Glendinning and Stefan Muthesius, *Tower Block*, Yale University Press, Yale, 1994, Chapters 4–8, 19, 22, 24 and pp 383–5, 391.
2. Ibid, pp 25–6; Walter Gropius, *The New Architecture and the Bauhaus*, MIT Press, 1934, 99ff.
3. Municipal Journal, 4 November 1955, pp 2985–89; Cleeve Barr, *Public Authority Housing*, 1958, pp 63–66; RIBA Journal, March 1955 (Symposium on High Flats).
4. London County Council, Housing Committee papers, 25 June 1952; Association of Building Technicians, Homes, 1946, p 48; *Architectural Design*, November 1951; Architect and Building News, 14 November 1947.
5. *Architectural Design*, September 1953; RIBA Journal, March 1955; for Corbusier influence and slabs, see Tower Block, op cit, pp 58, 385.
6. Sweden: *Tower Block*, pp 54–56, 385 (note 18). Roehampton: *Architectural Review*, July 1959; Nikolaus Pevsner, *The Englishness of English Art*, Penguin, London, 1956, pp 172–76; Living in Flats, 1–5; P Peters, Wohnhochhauser, Munich, c.1958, cited in *Architectural Design*, December 1958.
7. Gillian Ruth Owens, *Mixed Development in Local Authority Housing in England and Wales*, (PhD, London University), 1987; RIBA Journal, March 1955; *Tower Block*, op cit, pp 62, 385.
8. *Architectural Review*, January 1964; RIBA Journal, April 1962, pp. 156–57; Architects' Journal, 28 February 1962.
9. RIBA Journal, October 1965, pp499; *Architectural Design*, June 1955, p192; Architectural Design, February 1966, p 82; Builder, 28 July 1961, p 151.
10. PSSHAK: Architects' Journal, 15 September 1971; D Crawford (ed), *A Decade of Innovation in British Housing*, 1975, p 18; *Tower Block*, chapters 22, 24, 26.

In 1994, Miles Glendinning and Stefan Muthesius co-authored *Tower Block*, winner of the 1995 Alice Davis Hichcock Medallion for architectural history; the material in this article is drawn largely from that book.

feature to a social and architectural space in its own right, associated with a concept of English 'street community'. Initially adumbrated by Alison and Peter Smithson, the deck-access formula was put into large-scale practice at Sheffield Corporation's late 1950s Park Hill development (below), where it was combined with the Unité recipe of a variety of flat and maisonette types. In early 1960s projects such as Darbourne & Darke's Lillington Street development, Westminster, this type came under the influence of a growing dislike of straight, rectangular forms, and a desire for intricacy and private space. Now, the outside walls of the upper floor might be set back or projected out or 'staggered'. Staggered forms not only offered gains in lighting and privacy, but also the possibility of variations in dwelling sizes; the principle reached its logical extreme in pyramidal 'A-frame' megastructures, or (the opposite) inverted 'stadium' section developments such as Alexandra Road, Camden (from the late 1960s).[9]

'Open' Versus 'Closed' Systems
Most of these projects, despite their complexity, were associated with very precise, fixed architectural conceptions: there was little or no intention to allow for 'open-ended' flexibility in planning. That situation continued to prevail even during the years of 'industrialised building' in the 1960s, when some architects devoted much energy to proselytising a concept of 'open systems', based either on a fixed frame and flexible infill, or on a totally customisable structure of modular units. Despite their efforts, the 'open' ideal remained a pipe-dream; the

pragmatic emphasis, in reality, was on heavy, prefabricated 'closed systems', used mainly for the routine building of tower blocks, which reinforced the fixed and segmented house-plans.

The unattainability of the 'open systems' ideal in a mass-output context was underlined by the experience of two mid and late 1960s attempts to reconcile dwellings of varying unit sizes with heavy prefabrication systems, within the framework of an irregularly planned deck-access complex: the Yorkshire Development Group programme (architect: Martin Richardson), and the project at Gibson Street, Manchester (architect: Robert Stones/Manchester Development Group). Both these programmes had disastrous experiences of management and upkeep, and were demolished in the 1980s and early 1990s. The other potential variant of 'open systems', the frame and flexible-infill principle, had even less impact, and then solely in the field of low-rise housing. The only significant executed example was an experimental scheme built in 1970 in Hackney, London, by the Greater London Council; it was based on the PSSHAK (Primary System Support Housing and Assembly Kits) method devised by Professor NJ Habraken.[10]

Conclusion
Overall, the modernist social housing programmes in the UK refrained from revolutionary changes to the plan of the dwelling. In contrast to early Modern Movement propagandists, postwar public housing designers concentrated all their efforts to achieve free space on the exterior of the house, whether in the disposition of dwellings within blocks or in the layout of blocks within the wider urban ensemble; the abolition of compartmentalisation inside the house was never a serious aim. The 'transformation of the home' would instead be guaranteed by the provision of mod cons, and by building as many new houses as possible. 'Flexibility' in domestic planning was seen not in early modernist avant-garde terms, nor in post-1968 user-participation terms, but as a way of accommodating, by ad-hoc modifications to fairly conventional plans, the desires and worries of the real 'clients' of public housing design – the local politicians and administrators whose concern was to 'give the people homes'. Today, there are attempts to revive the formal vocabulary of postwar welfare-state architecture, perhaps in the hope that an imagery of 'community spirit' can help obscure the reality of the ongoing 'charitisation' and privatisation of social provision. But these spatial and theoretical aspects of the modernist heritage are of little relevance if divorced from the sheer scale of its ambition: this was a movement that proceeded not in experimental penny packets but on a colossal scale, 'transforming' the space of entire regions and nations with its plans and programmes. Ↄ

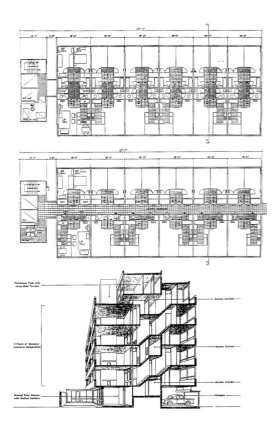

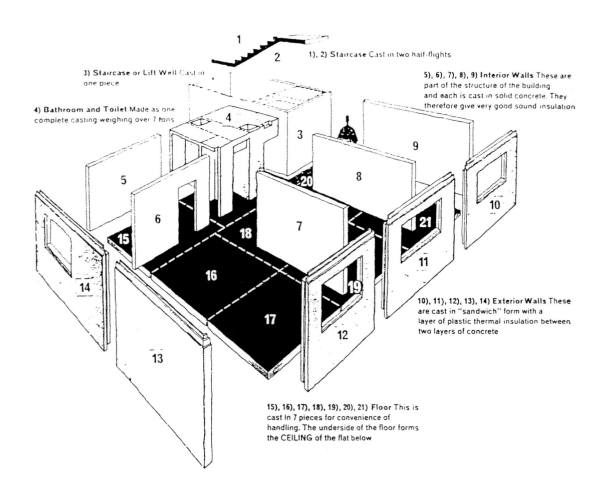

1), 2) Staircase Cast in two half-flights

3) Staircase or Lift Well Cast in one piece

4) Bathroom and Toilet Made as one complete casting weighing over 7 tons

5), 6), 7), 8), 9) Interior Walls These are part of the structure of the building and each is cast in solid concrete. They therefore give very good sound insulation

10), 11), 12), 13), 14) Exterior Walls These are cast in "sandwich" form with a layer of plastic thermal insulation between two layers of concrete

15), 16), 17), 18), 19), 20), 21) Floor This is cast in 7 pieces for convenience of handling. The underside of the floor forms the CEILING of the flat below

Transformable Architecture for the Homeless

Preening our domestic environment, making small alterations and changes in the way we use space, is often regarded as a privilege confined to the stable, comfortable and wealthy. In contrast to this, James Gallie explains why designers of emergency shelters for disaster areas should make the provision of future transformations – adaptations of dwellings by occupants and user participation – a priority.

Transformable dwellings for the homeless can be divided roughly into two kinds – those that are designed to transform, and those that are allowed to evolve. Either way, transformation is an inevitability when there is no home, and when emergency shelter is both a necessity and a guiding device for future transformation. This article looks at some of the critical sociological issues represented by existing situations as well as proposed technologies, and calls for an empathetic understanding of the needs of those who cannot afford to choose.

'Homelessness' is a term that can be adopted to cover all conditions in which the understanding of place is in flux and therefore of critical importance. It is a situation invariably brought about by force of circumstance and involves not only the lack of secure shelter but also the loss of a place of settlement and security – the home, land, village or city. Each situation is different and requires localised consideration. Awareness of this has led to greater emphasis on self-help mechanisms as an ethical response.[1] The sociological and political arguments for and against self-help are evenly matched and far from straightforward in their path towards resolution.[2] As with much humanitarian discourse, they are both informed and interrupted by the perceived need for rapid response and emergency relief. On the ground, aid packages tend to fall back on donor-led, economically accountable solutions that fail to consider either the complexities of a situation or the current praxis in humanitarian discourse, which itself tends towards inflexible blanket theory. Appropriate technology and transformability become bywords for a cautionary approach that attempts to navigate the rocky channels between active and passive intervention, between short-term relief and long-term assistance, between steering development and not knowing the future.

Evolution–Transformation

Whilst the assumption that victims of disaster require aid is irrefutable, we have much to learn from communities that have established themselves, either through necessity caused by forced homelessness in exile, or through the growth of outer-urban regions, shanty towns and slums. The Gaza Strip, for example, remains one of the most densely populated regions of the world and like many such areas it is still growing. The first generation of refugees from the establishment of Israel, often reasonably wealthy and educated, were allowed to settle in camps which, three generations on, and with freedom to leave Gaza denied to all but a few Palestinians, now have a population of around a quarter of a million, housed in a density unimaginable in most modern cities. Despite the lack of effective planning, external assistance or resources, and the strongly held desire to return home, houses in the camps have grown out of both fundamental need and memory. New rooms are built for growing families, party walls are shared and maintained, doors open off narrow streets – the domain of children – into almost tranquil courtyards with tiled floors and perhaps a small tree for shade. More important still are the carried objects such as keys, pictures and tools which, given a proper place, transform the shelter into a place of greater meaning. Using recovered concrete blocks and corrugated metal, these places show signs of an evolution that shares more with the villages of the Peloponese than many of the carefully planned camps established by the United Nations High Commission for Refugees and other relief agencies across the globe. Gaza provides evidence of a phenomenon that many architects and planners may have suspected with a resigned nihilism – that places of meaning can only really be completed by occupants or users and that the designer, although a necessity in modern urban conditions, may be interfering with the evolutionary place-making process.

Solutions for Kosovo

Despite the sensitivity of places such as Gaza, basic services planning is essential for the avoidance of sprawling, uncontrolled and unhygienic slums. Homeless communities are invariably forced to start from scratch in rebuilding themselves, often away from destroyed homes and in conditions of political and social adversity. Such situations compress the time scale of development. 'Top down' housing provision is both subject to, and may be

Right
Camps, the Gaza Strip, 1997

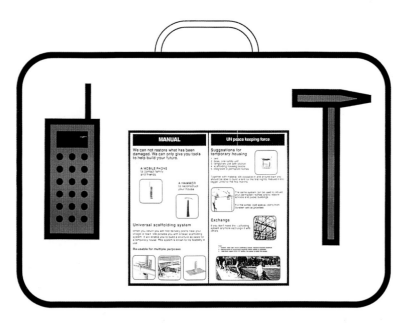

partially responsible for, social instability. A middle ground must be sought between natural evolution and controlled transformation – planning is critical, and decisions should look first at the economic, social and cultural reality before implementing any form of built technology. The challenge of proposing solutions for this dilemma was met by many of the entries in the 'Architecture for Humanity' exhibition of solutions for returnees to Kosovo. This exhibition grew out of a competition open to professionals and nonprofessionals all over the world and the number of entries was spectacular. The broad aim was to find appropriate technologies and strategies that would provide low-cost shelter without compromising long-term redevelopment.

The return of many Kosovars to their homeland after much of it had been destroyed created a rare situation of repatriation. It could be assumed that people would wish to return to their homes, but since many found them destroyed, and have lost members of their family and community, it is difficult to predict the shifting that is likely to take place over the next few years. A number of the entries suggested a belief that these people are more than capable of handling their situation given the basic provisions of modern existence. Ruimtelab and Linders en Van Dorssen's compelling entry revolved around the provision of packages containing a mobile phone, a hammer, and a set of instructions similar to emergency- exit guides in passenger aircraft. These instructions locate depots for scaffolding and provisions. Building materials can then be traded as shelters become homes, storage facilities or

shops. Ideologically, the technology and approach allows for flux without narrowing choice or opportunity. With a system of registration, people could find each other by name or profession and the vital catalysts of reparation are already in place – communication, information and choice. Gone are segregation, dictated solutions and top-down intervention. In this way, transformation enables redevelopment following the provision, rather than imposition, of shelter and aid. Like many suggestions, this idea should not be taken too literally, although it suggests an awareness of some of the sociological issues, such as the evolution of shelter, upon which planners and designers should be basing their ideas.

Other entries replaced this flexible approach to future development with particular technologies, and thus varying levels of dependence on design and assistance, which in many real situations have proved unreliable in the long term. A common proposal was the reuse of rubble from destroyed buildings in gabian walls, or blocks using supplied wire mesh for fast, self-buildable houses. Others suggested the use of cargo containers as shelters, which could be transformed into homes by stacking them up and adding windows, doors and roofs. These containers utilise a common infrastructure and are about the right size for one or two people. However, as with the houses built using gabian technology, it is likely that inhabitants will not want to live in these structures for ever, although containers could be used as temporary shelters whilst permanent homes were built or rebuilt nearby, or shelters were prefabricated to the same size as the containers to utilise the same infrastructure. Less cumbersome suggestions involved intermediate or high-tech provisions that could enable evolution, such as paper-tube houses, wood palettes, super-adobe, strawbale walls and timber or steel-frame structures, which could be fleshed out with locally available materials, either natural or artificial.

These solutions are bound together ideologically by the need to transform through time. This could mean growth or movement, physical or social change. Apart from the solution from the Netherlands, all display a common trait, which may be taken for granted in countries where designed environments are bought and sold as commodities, but is problematic in places such as Kosovo, where such solutions are imposed. Something has to be fixed – either the technology itself or the rules that govern its transformation. This places constraints on transformation – a house can change into an office or shop, a wall can move to become a roof or a table, but the locus of its movement is carefully designed and by default its future transformation is contained within the parameters of availability in the marketplace and skilled assistance. Refugee camps may evolve from tents into dwellings into homes, but refugees are prevented from moving into the city and forced to depend on aid distribution, supplied food and resources. Self-build schemes utilise appropriate materials (not necessarily local) but the pattern for construction and growth is established by humanitarian organisations. This form of we-design-you-build simply sanctions the use of un-unionised low-wage labour without necessarily increasing basic rights or self-sufficiency.

The Space Frame
The need to understand the sociological issues at play in architecture generally and housing provision particularly, was of critical importance in the work of Yona Friedman. Friedman published a manifesto, 'L'Architecture Mobile', in the 1960s, setting out details of what he called *la ville spatiale*. These were huge superstructures within which inhabitants were allowed to construct their own homes. Friedman's *L'Architecture Mobile* epitomised the late modernist fascination with

physical structures, social housing and the developing awareness of, and concern for, global issues such as rising populations and poverty. In these schemes, hollow supporting structures or skeletons raised above ground level would contain all services such as wiring and water. The occupants of the frames could then make any spatial arrangement through the placement of mobile partitions, walls and floor slabs.[3] Friedman's drawings exhibit an unquestioning belief that a strong framework (in his case, literally) could be used to facilitate self-help where housing is required. The space frame in the sky is analogous to society, and the dwellings therein the products of individuality. The driving belief is that individuality and temporal transformation should be characterised and enabled in the built environment. At the same time, growing and moving populations need to be controlled, ideally by floating above the planet, touching it as little as possible. The space frame refers, therefore, not just to the physical potential of large-span structures, but to the sociologically opposing connotations of the words 'space' (freedom and individuality) and 'frame' (society and control).

This construction was the result of a Transitional Housing Construction Workshop organised by Spacex Gallery, Exeter, in conjunction with the exhibition 'HOMING: projects for Kosovo'. Using simple building materials, including gabions, rubble and metal foil, Mike Lawless of LDA Architects worked with homeless men from Gabriel House, pupils from Barley Lane School, Exeter, and foundation course students from Exeter College to build this shelter. The HOMING exhibition brought together artists' and architects' projects, searching for solutions related to the massive upheaval following the Kosovan crisis. The exhibition assisted the work of charities like Warchild, who have broad experience of working in countries and communities devastated by conflict.

The Issue of Transformation

Friedman's superstructures form a utopian environment where the single individual rather than the average human is given scope to find and create his or her place in society. This vision is similar to that of many entries in 'Architecture for Humanity', where the immediacy of the situation demanded a degree of empathy for the dispossessed Kosovans and sensitive solutions for their plight. The exhibition highlighted the growing awareness that many designed solutions cannot fail to dictate design development and thus take degrees of choice away from the user. Some solutions, such as the Aluminium House by Blaser and Morath in Switzerland, avoided the complex issues surrounding self-help and resorted to the 'power politics' of a top-

down and easily accountable intervention by way of prefabricating entire houses in Switzerland.

Between the Swiss and Dutch solutions lies the spectrum of technology, from low tech to high tech and from less accountable 'bottom-up' to accountable top-down solutions. All these technologies imply varying degrees of flexibility but also impose limits on the user or inhabitant. In wealthy societies, the desire for transformation may be for good reason. Presented with infinite choice but having lost the ability to find guidance in nature or necessity, we succumb to the forces of consumerism. The sociology of the house in wealthy liberal societies is, in a sense, a reversal of the situation in Gaza. In the former case, transformability in the domestic realm may be analogous to increasing instability, the development of information technology and the resulting decline or reshaping of liberal-democratic notions of place. In the latter case (and for much of the world), transformable houses are simply a necessity. The paradox is that the needs of the homeless are not necessarily in opposition to those of liberal-democratic or technological cultures, as the two may be closer than the images of suffering presented by the media, for example in Bosnia Herzegovina, Kobe, Turkey, Chechenya and Kosovo, lead us to believe. Amongst other things, the legacy of colonialism is that we have tended to assume that victims of natural or man-made disaster are necessarily demoted to Third World status and they are implicitly treated as such by humanitarian organisations. Disaster has an unerring ability to erase history and promote notions of 'the sentimental order', which in turn gives rise to 'charity cannibalism' whereby pity and compassion are exchanged for the spectacle of the destitution of others.[4] Awareness of this must be maintained without the withdrawal of proactive involvement. It is an awareness that should shape the architect's involvement from the sociological roots of design and provision to the promotion of technology that facilitates the creation of place.

Just as Marc Auge characterised non-places as places of transit, by extension, the transformable home is a contradiction in terms – it is a destabilised place, and therefore not a place.[5] Instead, it is a physical extension of destabilised identity as manipulated by fashion, products, images and information (chosen impositions) as well as memory and daily life (personal and transcendent). Those fortunate enough to be able to enjoy this 'ferociously

Darwinian' environment and to subordinate technology, or who passively assume its necessity, can buy into an ever-changing existence.[6] Indeed transformation, movement and flux invariably result either from choice and expenditure or from force and necessity. These opposing reasons for transformation ostensibly characterise the difference between mobility within self-defined parameters, and homelessness. Likewise, the technology presupposed by common notions of the transformable dwelling can either be subordinated to the desire for an ever-changing life, or can unwittingly subordinate the unfortunate victims of war or disaster.

There cannot be a formula for good housing provision, which is independent of social empathy. It is possible that wealthy societies are moving away from living conditions based on class or historically based identity and towards conditions that represent and exhibit flexibility. The only common denominator is freedom and wealth. As this occurs, rather than patronise the less fortunate we may empathise with their sociological needs. For example, as the social housing projects of the 1950s and 1960s are gradually being sold off, their value in the marketplace is becoming more apparent and this is forcing us to re-evaluate what makes a successful building. In London, high-rise blocks are transformed from icons of social decay into desirable vertical villages, which work as they were intended – providing spacious accommodation elevated above the city, without social hierarchy. The essence seems to be rights of ownership and the freedom to choose. There was never anything inherently wrong with many of these buildings other than what they represented.

The obvious alternative to consumer choice where there is no money and no market, is user participation, either in construction or design depending on the situation. Moreover, like a tree, the successful growth of a home can be ensured by careful planting. It needs a good start, in the right soil and conditions. The satisfaction of planting is tempered if, later on, the tree dies because the planting has been hastily done. A home will develop if, like a tree, its roots are secure. This gives rise to desirable transformation irrespective of the chosen technology. Like Yona Friedman, the architect should be an engineer, a sociologist and an economist. He or she should be able to coordinate the skills of technicians with the desires of the community and should listen more than dictate. Of course, difficult decisions have to be made, but they should always be informed. In continually shifting situations such as homeless communities and resettlement programmes, such a role implies constant involvement with less predetermined design so that places can evolve like cities and towns, and fundamentally strive towards the stability and security of home. ⌂

Notes
1. See J Turner, Housing by People , Marion Boyars, London.
2. See R Burgess in P Ward, Self Help Housing – A Critique, Mansell London, 1982, p 23.
3. Yona Friedman, Structures Servicing the Unpredictable Nai, Publications, Rotterdam, 1999. Such schemes are comparable to 'Sites and Services' projects for refugee camps and housing projects, where everything but the shelter is provided.
4. Christopher Horrocks, Baudrillard and the Millennium, Icon Books, London, 1999. See also W J Mitchell, City of Bits, Space, Place and the Infobahn, MIT Press (Cambridge, Mass), 1995.
5. Marc Auge, Non-Places. Introduction to an Anthropology of Supermodernity, Verso, 1995, p 94.
6. Mitchell, op cit, p 4.

David Thorpe's Collages

Many of the greatest leaps in the architectural imagination, such as those of Piranesi, have been explored in artworks. Catherine Wood looks at the work of contemporary artist David Thorpe, who creates virtual cityscapes out of rearranged fractured views of south London, drawn from his own memory. He transforms mundane urban features such as skate parks and tower blocks, infusing them with glamour and romance. The physical process of cutting and pasting small fragments of paper in order to compose the pictures is integral to this concept.

'Just what is it that makes today's homes so different, so appealing?' was the question posed by Richard Hamilton's famous collage, created as an advertisement for the Whitechapel Art Gallery's 'This is Tomorrow' exhibition in 1956. Another work in the exhibition, by Alison and Peter Smithson, combined cut and pasted magazine pictures with architectural drawings to display their proposal for the Golden Lane housing estate in the East End of London. Thomas Crow points to the snaking vacuum cleaner hose in Hamilton's collage as symbolic of the 'ruling order' of consumerism, which is 'impossible extension'. The same phrase might be applied to the structural frames that enabled the Smithson's proposal to be made concrete.

It comes as no surprise, then, to learn that contemporary artist David Thorpe has been looking at 1950s editions of *Progressive Architecture*. In his earlier works, he appears spellbound by those impossible extensions of the house. He constructs striking cityscapes that show how it might have been. Silhouetted figures gaze in awe at soaring tower blocks and flyovers, bold and clean-cut against bright blue heavens. Occasionally, fireworks pierce the night sky, shooting almost as high as the lit windows of the upper storeys. The natural elements, either choked by concrete or tamed into recreational display, have little chance of featuring in these city scenes.

In recent work, however, Thorpe looks outside the areas yoked by human habitation and we begin to understand the simultaneous fantasy of awesomeness and control fulfilled by those urban landscapes. It is only against the backdrop of the Friedrich-esque 'real outdoors' that such human aspirations begin to look faintly ridiculous. The appeal of the planned 119-metre Chiswick 'Pinnacle' is perhaps little different in essence from that of the sheer cliff face at which caravan dwellers gawk in *We are Majestic in the Wilderness* (1999).

It is impossible not to wonder at Thorpe's intricately constructed cities of the mind. But like all idealised plans – and like the estates in south east London to which they refer, seen from an overland train at twilight – they look perfect from a distance. It is only when you look close up that you see the disease. Thorpe's figures might look contented and safe sharing the public spaces of the expanded domestic skin, but the surfaces of his works are agitated, allergic. You cannot ignore the process: the painstaking cutting and pasting of a million tiny pieces. There is an obsessive quality to the work that jars with its romantic subject and highlights that which drives the longing for a clear, omniscient vista. The high-rise transformed domestic sphere cannot offer this: Thorpe has to make it for himself.

Opposite
David Thorpe: *We are Majestic in the Wilderness* (paper cut-out 183x152.5 cm) 1997.
Left
David Thorpe: *Kings of the Night* (paper cut-out 155x163 cm) 1997.

Jestico + Whiles

A House for the Future

Jestico + Whiles' competition-winning design for 'A House for the Future' is currently being built by Redrow Homes at the Museum of Welsh Life in St Fagan's, Cardiff. Due for completion in the autumn of 2000, the house will open to the public in the spring 2001 and will form part of the museum's collection of over 40 original buildings moved from various parts of Wales, and re-erected to form live, outdoor exhibits. The house will take its place in the museum's collection as a natural evolution of traditional Welsh housing, responding to local conditions, climate and the availability of materials. Here, Heinz Richardson and Jude Harris of Jestico + Whiles, a practice with a long association with contemporary sustainable design, describe how their design caters for the living patterns of tomorrow's world and employs a strategy of sensible energy-use and passive technologies. BBC Wales, who are collaborating with the National Museums and Galleries of Wales on this project, will film a family 'test driving' the house for a week before it is opened to the public.

It is possible that in less than a lifetime, all human enterprise will be modelled upon the behaviour and characteristics of natural systems. The conventional ideas of traditional family life and consumer-led enterprise will be challenged by an exponential increase in the necessity to embrace the issues of sustainability. These issues will affect not only our environment and the way in which we interact with it, but also our socioeconomic structures. The conventional model based on the nuclear family of two adults and 2.4 children is increasingly becoming obsolete, replaced by more dynamic, short-term structures responding to changes in economic circumstance and driven by technological change and an increasing desire for flexibility.

The boundaries between working and home life are also becoming blurred. Notions of the home office are now commonplace as the information revolution opens up an ever-increasing range of possibilities. This dynamic, fast-moving rate of change will place increasing demands on our homes to be flexible and responsive to changes in family structure, work patterns, technological advance and other innovations. If a house is flexible enough to double as a work space, then this serves to reduce the need for commuting long distances to work, and thus unnecessary transport emissions.

The design for 'A House for the Future' is based on all of these principles. Embracing sustainability and flexibility as key determinants of form, it provides a model for future housing, capable of reproduction and repetition in a multitude of configurations, in many different locations. It has been conceived both as offering a rural or suburban model on greenfield sites with detached units, or one for a higher density terrace, more appropriate to urban brownfield sites.

It has been designed to be within the reach of an average house-buying budget. There was a desire to make the house buildable at a price of approximately £40,000 per structural bay, allowing numerous variations with a simple price tag in space terms: for example, a two-bay model for £80,000.

The modular layout provides a simple structure designed to enclose flexible space, which can be adapted over time to suit changing life style and circumstance. The house will eschew high-energy technology and embrace appropriate sustainable technologies incorporated within a contemporary design.

Sustainability

It is well known that buildings consume over half the world's energy and a significant amount is also used in the manufacture of construction materials. The other dominant consumers are transport and industry, whose activities are closely associated with buildings and their location. We are faced with an impending environmental crisis if we do not slow down the reversal of photosynthesis that results from combustion (the burning of fossil fuels). As major consumers of energy, it is imperative that the burden buildings place on the world's finite resources is reduced. The future of our environment depends on innovations in low- or zero-emission buildings and on an environmentally responsible transport system.

One of the most significant contributions that buildings can make to the reduction of greenhouse-gas emissions is to reduce their consumption of non-renewable resources through energy efficiency and improved conservation. Direct energy uses have been minimised within the House for the Future, as has the embodied energy of the materials used in construction; the latter has been achieved by specifying local materials. The site offers ample potential for the growth of food and a secure cycle store has been provided to encourage sustainable transport use.

Energy

The House for the Future relies on a strategy of sensible energy use, assisted by passive technologies that are supported by easy-to-use control systems. It has been designed to be interactive with both its occupants and visitors, with provision for maximum user-control. When solar gain is insufficient, space heating can be supplemented by the ground-source heat pump and at the highest peaks of demand a pellet wood-burning stove can heat the space. Roof-mounted solar collectors will be able to provide water-heating for most of the year. Provision has also been made for electricity to be generated by a ridge-mounted wind generator and an integral photovoltaic array to meet some of the household's electricity demand. The intention is for the house to become self-sufficient in electricity as energy-generating technologies become more affordable.

Space heating is supplied to the house by an electric ground-source heat pump fed from a 35-metre borehole. This system was chosen because no mains gas is available to the site. The heat pump is intended to be powered by electricity from renewable sources, which would equate to zero carbon-dioxide emissions. In the medium term, this is achieved by purchasing electricity through 'green tariffs', which offer renewably generated electricity at a premium rate. Heat pumps using electricity work in the same way as a conventional refrigerator, which takes unwanted heat from food and releases it from cooling fins: the heat pump takes heat from the ground and releases it as useful warmth in the house. The system installed in this house is 315 per cent efficient: each unit of electricity delivered can produce 3.15 units of heat. High levels of insulation and high-performance glazing throughout help to minimise heat loss from the building, thus reducing the need for artificial heat input.

Water
Rainwater falling on the north-facing roof is collected in the oversized eaves gutter, which can store more than 3 cubic metres of water at high level. This can then be fed by gravity for various functions within the house, such as toilet flushing and the washing machine. This water is mechanically filtered to remove particles and is used for all 'non contact' requirements in the house. The house will collect an average of 155 litres per day, which is equal to about 56 cubic metres per year (about 25 per cent of an average family's annual water consumption). Other water-saving features include low-flush WCs, low-water appliances and aerated 'mousser' taps.

Materials
The structure of the house consists of a post-and-beam timber frame prefabricated with locally grown oak. A super-insulated wall of timber studwork 'wraps' around three sides of the building, allowing maximum flexibility for window and door openings. This is faced externally with lime render and oak boarding. The void between the timbers is filled with 200 millimetres of sheep's wool insulation.

Internally, flexibility is provided by non-loadbearing timber studwork partitions. The concrete ground-slab, containing recycled aggregate, provides useful thermal mass to regulate the passive solar gain. Additional thermal mass is also provided by earth-block partitions on the ground floor, which were manufactured on site using clay fill found there. All materials were selected with consideration for low embodied energy.

The north-facing roof will be covered with sedum plants laid on a recycled aluminium roof. It also

ŷ ar gyfer y dyfodol, amgueddfa werin cymru, sain ffagan *a house for the future, museum of welsh life, st fagans*

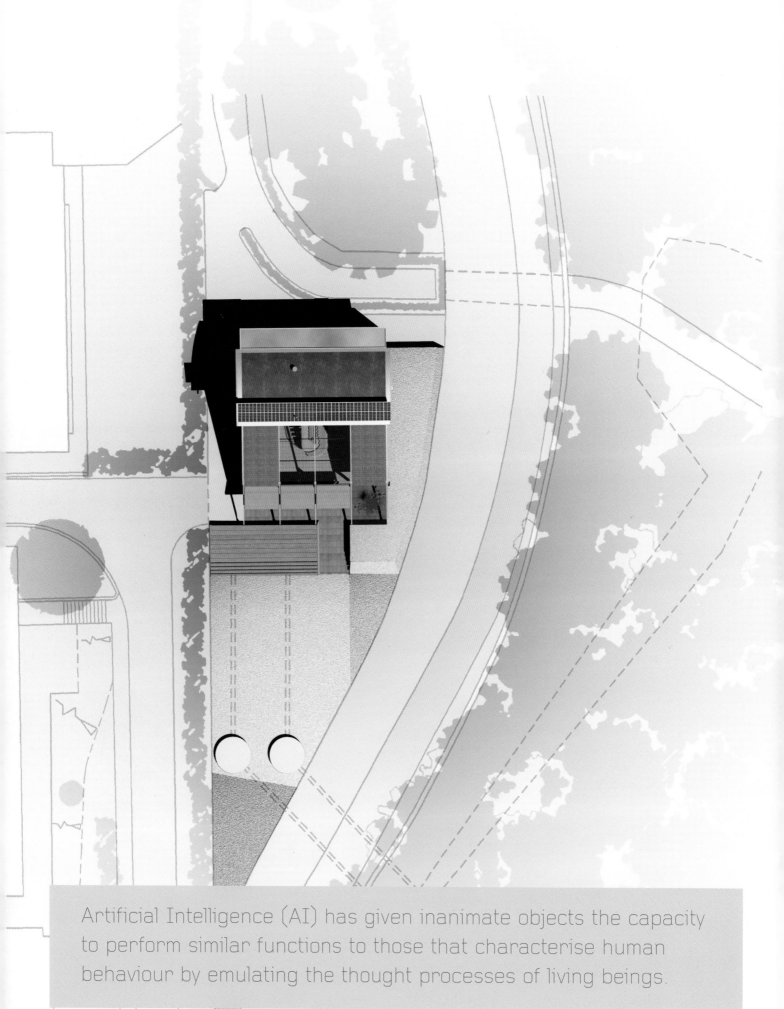

Artificial Intelligence (AI) has given inanimate objects the capacity to perform similar functions to those that characterise human behaviour by emulating the thought processes of living beings.

contains cellulose-fibre insulation between the rafters. The insulation is made from recycled newspapers, books and telephone directories, and is treated with borax as a flame and insect retardant. This approach to 'greening' the roof was chosen as a more cost-effective and environmentally responsible solution, than using turf as turf roofs are often very heavy and require significant amounts of synthetic materials to keep the water out of the interior.

Adaptive and Responsive

The House for the Future has been designed as an Intelligent Home. The word 'intelligent' implies the possession of intellectual faculties that provide a capacity for understanding. Artificial Intelligence (AI) has given inanimate objects the capacity to perform similar functions to those that characterise human behaviour by emulating the thought processes of living beings. Intelligent Buildings are high-technology manifestations, stacked high with gadgetry. The House for the Future will incorporate some 'intelligent' devices and appliances that will assist in the efficient operation of the house. Home automation of this type offers significant advantages to the disabled, who can benefit from automatically controlled devices. Perhaps more importantly, though, the house has been designed to be 'responsive', emulating systems seen in nature, such as the thermoregulatory powers of the human skin, the seasonal changes of coat for many mammals and the opening and closing of flowers in response to sunlight.

Buildings can be seen as the interface between the occupant and the varying climatic conditions throughout the day and between seasons, as a means of protection from the extremes of climate. A building is a static, inanimate object that moves only slightly in response to structural and thermal stresses. An element of variability is required to reverse this inertia and give a building the capacity to respond dynamically to the variations of climate, occupancy and time.

Such dynamism is found in the House for the Future and is provided by particular elements. For example, opening windows and variable levels of insulation on the south-facing glazing allow controllable passive solar gain daily and seasonally. These glazed elements are designed to change according to the seasons of the year in the same way that human beings moderate the body's capacity to store or lose heat by increasing/decreasing the wearing of layers of thermally efficient clothing. To further reduce night-time and cold-weather loss of heat through the south-facing glazing, a motorised roller blind will be mounted internally to act like an 'overcoat' to the building, providing a responsive skin to the most vulnerable internal areas. This dynamic protection system can also reduce unwanted solar gain in the height of summer and protect the interior in the depth of winter. Additionally, it will reduce and soften the 'black hole' effect associated with glazing exposed to the night sky. Surrounding vegetation will also provide a form of variable shading and protection from the elements.

Planning of the internal living space is kept deliberately fluid to respond to the particular needs of the residents both now and in the future. Open living and daytime spaces are located to the south, whilst more private and enclosed cellular spaces are located on the northern side of the dwelling. The modular approach to the design of the house allows the possibility for a number of variations to the base model according to spatial needs, a desire for flexibility and available finance. A simple shell structure can be increasingly colonised or cellularised as the circumstances of the residents alter with time and economics. The house can be conceived as either a 'loft on the ground', or more cellularised to suit family life. The number of bedrooms can vary from one to five in various modular configurations, with the option of a 'granny flat', teenagers' den or sublet apartment as required. Opportunities for extending the 'extruded' section are infinite. ∆

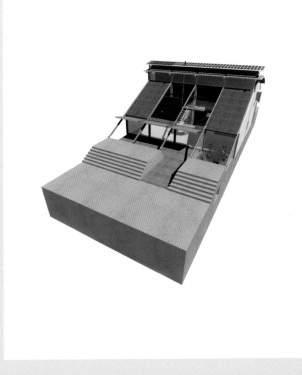

The MIT Home of the Future

House_n

The unending search for the shape of the future has challenged the minds of fantasists and visionaries since the early days of popular science fiction. For futurologists, the years ahead have been symbolised by aerocars, monorails, sub-Atlantic tunnels, meals-in-a-pill and, above all, a technological revolution in the domestic environment. The house of the future has been the subject of popular science, from sci-fi comics like the Eagle, to television programmes such as *Tomorrow's World*, which have taken note of the full-scale visions realised at world's fairs and trade shows throughout the twentieth century. Often shaped like mushrooms and constructed from bizarre new materials such as plastic, these future homes have offered a plethora of labour-saving devices and automation; a space-age environment in which technology and everyday life are totally integrated.

MIT departments, including the School of Architecture and Planning, the renowned Media Lab and the Department of Mechanical Engineering, as well as the Harvard Medical School.

Described as a 'contextual and physical context' in which to investigate solutions for future dwellings, House_n is more than a simple show home. Attempting to provide a broad overview of the way in which technological transformations will alter our living patterns in the near future, House_n's concerns include ensuring that housing technology will encompass the massive transgenerational change created by the ageing postwar baby boomers, providing homes that will facilitate independence for an increasingly elderly population.

However, it is in the realm of creating 'adaptable, customisable environments' that House_n most closely approaches a purely technological approach to transformable architecture. The House_n programme emphasises the integration of computation and

Towards the end of the twentieth century, the future home was no longer a test-bed for wacky forms and way-out architecture, and style had become secondary to technology.

But over the years, there has been a sea change in how the house of the future is conceived. Towards the end of the twentieth century, the future home was no longer a test-bed for wacky forms and way-out architecture, and style had become secondary to technology. The push-button future retreated behind brick facades and mock-Tudor cladding, as house builders opted for a conservative suit for their silicon innovations. Although the 1990s saw a resurgence in futuristic, speculative architectural studies, most notably in the area of sustainable and environmentally friendly design, the housing industry has remained, for the most part, unadventurous. There have been few attempts to tie in the latest technological developments to a flexible form of domestic architecture that allows not only for customisation by individual owners, but can also adapt to the swiftly changing world of technology.

An example of an attempt to meld futuristic technology with futuristic style is House_n, developed by a multidisciplinary team at the Massachusetts Institute of Technology. The programme, led by Kent Larson and Chris Luebekeman, involves several

architecture, not only through enhancing traditional electrical systems in housing, such as heating, communication, entertainment, but also through new construction materials, user interfaces, availability of information (through permanent Internet connections) and adaptability to changing use. This might even occur at the design stage, merging CAD technology with the views of real-estate agents to allow for true 'customisation'. Once built, House_n could be defined as 'intelligent', whether through the use of sensors and 'fuzzy logic' to ensure heating controls are always at their most efficient, shutting down unused rooms, automatically ventilating areas, etc, or via the ubiquity of the Web – providing educational resources for example.

The 'Internet home' has, in the past two years, become a virtual cliché. It usually takes the form of a conventional show home stuffed with net-enabled PCs and webcams to allow families to shop, work and chat to each other from all over the house. But this technology appears superfluous when applied to contemporary living patterns. House_n's multidisciplinary origins, coupled with MIT's reputation as a futuristic think-tank, should provide a more realistic template for transformability through technology. ◲ *Jonathan Bell*

Hinged Space

(from Autonomous to Interactive)

The epitome of the transformable is the moving and the dynamic. Steven Holl's notion of 'hinged space', as he explains here, is both interactive and movable. It is exemplified by his built work. His housing for Fukuoka in Japan has rooms with removable corners and rotating walls.

Adjustable space comes alive, especially in the domestic arenas of Manhattan or Tokyo, where every square metre is a universe. Beyond autonomous, room-by-room space, is interactive space. 'Participating walls' reorder domestic environments. Space can be dynamic and contingent.

Around 1983, Steven Holl Architects began to experiment with hinged space in a series of apartment designs in Manhattan (the Cohen apartment and X-Y-Z apartment in the MOMA Tower, and the THEO-LOGICAL apartment). The then-current polemics of deconstruction led to twisted grids, shards of walls, tortured folds, etc. When these geometries were built, space was frozen into a caricature of the dynamic, static in realisation.

In Fukuoka, Japan, the client, Fukuoka Jisho, asked us to provide 28 two-, three- and four-bedroom apartments. We returned to Japan with our presentation in 1989, conservatively proposing that half the apartments would use experimental 'hinged space', while the other half would be more normative, with bedrooms. After an oriental silence, one of the 30

Opposite
Void space/hinged space
housing, Fukuoka 1989–91:
interior, hinged space, open.

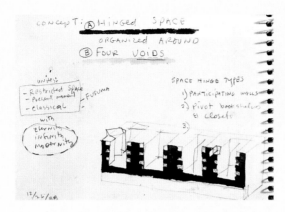

Top
Void space/hinged space
housing, Fukuoka 1989–91:
watercolour, concept sketch.

Middle
Watercolour, concept sketch.

Bottom
Exterior view.

Right
Void space/hinged space
housing, Fukuoka 1989–91:
interior.

dark-suited Japanese said firmly, 'Make them all hinged space!' Japan was to become an architect's heaven. We realised 28 apartments in hinged space. Each was different, organised in several hinged-space types – interlocking like a Chinese puzzle around four 'void' water courts. In some cases, entire room corners were pulled away with rotating walls. The hinged-space dynamics allowed an interactive reformation of the entire domestic arena. Domestic life changed with the space in diurnal, perennial and episodic cycles.

In 1994, I collaborated with Vito Acconci on the design for the Storefront for Art and Architecture in Manhattan. The interactive, dynamic facade established the argument of an inside-out facade, which addressed insular art and turned it to the public street. With Vito's energy and ideas, hinged space was transformed to rotate on both axes, which allowed some walls to become tables and benches. Interactive space like this can be exact and precise in one variation and suddenly evolve into dynamic combinatory space. Rather than being pure or minimal, this space is crossbred. It can be severe or easygoing. When the facade is closed, it takes on the typological form of a triangular slice of shopfront, typical of Manhattan. When the facade is open, it becomes topological, drawing in the city outside. From a three-dimensional volume, it can be transformed into a four-dimensional landscape that changes in time. The body is linked to the wall forms in the crude sense that the shoulder is needed to push space out or pull it in. Incompleteness and open indeterminacy was established in multiple, informal order. Storefront was a breakthrough in realising dynamic, urban, interactive space, even though the entire budget for this project was equal to just one custom-made carpet for an Upper Eastside apartment. The dynamic, hinged-space gallery walls have been used as screens for digital projection installations. Merging space-time and information, one of the exhibitions, 'The 220 Minute Museum', by Hani Rashid and his Columbia students, stretched the little space even further into a real-virtual bridge – digitally operative as an experimental probe – a non-linear, interactive opening beyond hinged space. ☒

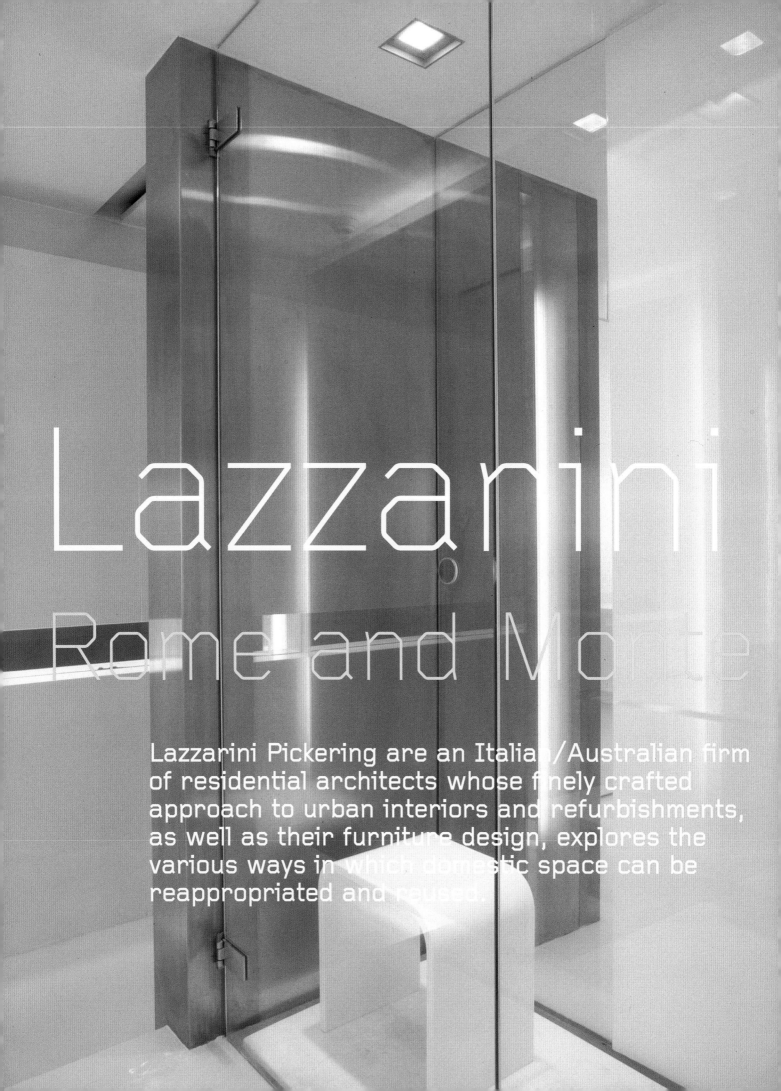

Lazzarini
Rome and Monte

Lazzarini Pickering are an Italian/Australian firm of residential architects whose finely crafted approach to urban interiors and refurbishments, as well as their furniture design, explores the various ways in which domestic space can be reappropriated and reused.

Pickering
Carlo Apartments

The architects collaborate closely with their clients
to ensure that a project fits entirely with their wishes.
The firm has also worked on refurbishments for the
Monaco-based yacht firm Wally, an area in which
design solutions must be ingenious configurations
of small spaces using innovative storage design.

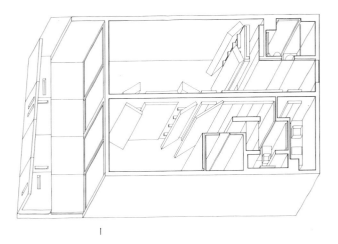

I

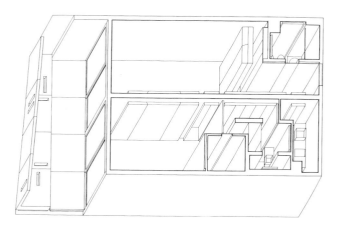

Rome Apartment 1994-95

This project is described by the architects as 'the portrait of the client' – a busy young woman in the fashion world – and was driven from the beginning by her very clear idea for a Japanese house in Rome. Over time, Lazzarini Pickering came to understand that her house would form a necessary component of a consciously chosen and ritualised way of living. Their literal references to indigenous Japanese architecture have elucidated the practice's own interest and research into transformable spaces and the delineation of functions.

The site was a small, vernacular house near the Pantheon, where a hotchpotch of structural Band Aids had been applied to myriad problems over time. Lazzarini Pickering definitively resolved the structural issues and began to articulate the space according to three dynamic 'functional and formal centres': the bath and the western dining table, the door/desk/work surface for the kitchen, and the night table, which incorporated rotating drawers and an extractable bench. Black-glass mosaic distinguishes service spaces (entrance, bath, kitchen) from the bleached-oak parquet of the other zones. Sliding Perspex panels were incorporated to open up and close off vistas and circulation spaces throughout the house. The movement of these elements, coupled with strong design ideas governing intensities of artificial lighting, contribute to create an environment that is infinitely variable. Lazzarini Pickering state that although the architect and client have only 'partially explored' the configurations this enables, they enjoy the fact that the project 'hides even to its designers something of itself'.

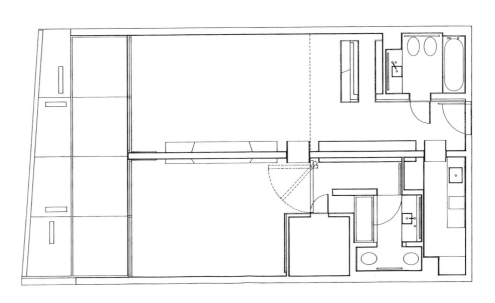

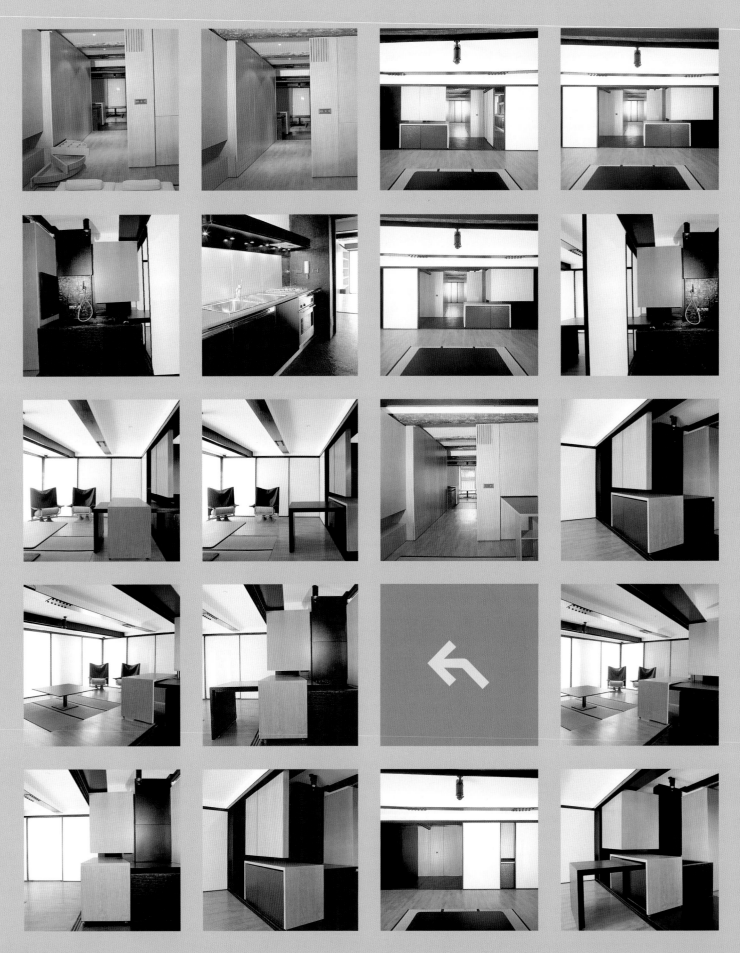

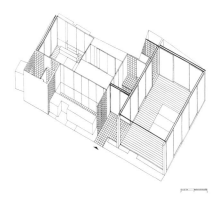

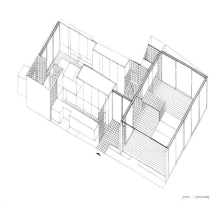

Monte Carlo Apartment, 1997

Lazzarini Pickering's brief, for a businessman who spends a few days a week in Monaco, was simply to design a 'beautiful hotel room', purposefully separate from family life and entertaining . Their client gave them free reign and did not meet them during the design process, talking only over the telephone. Perhaps inspired by this mysterious approach, the primary concrete loadbearing wall has been broken down into elements that serve to conjure, trick and surprise: glowing shelving units lit internally by coloured gelatin lights; a swivelling mirrored surface producing an infinite variety of reflected images and vistas; portals lined in stainless steel. These are glamorous interventions, verging on kitsch. The kitchen, bathrooms and wardrobes were inserted as pure volumes into
the shell of the apartment, and the balcony has been treated as an integral interior space. A panoramic view over the bay is framed by a slicing, horizontal aperture, which returns into the solid flank wall in a strip of reflective material. This 'dissolves' the wall by appearing as a continuation of the window – blue by day and black at night. Lazzarini Pickering felt able to utilise delicate materials that would not normally withstand the rough and tumble of everyday family life and, besides the glamorous undertones, the overwhelming impression of the project is of an elegant and peaceful interior, a haven from a hectic schedule. **Δ** *Sally Godwin*

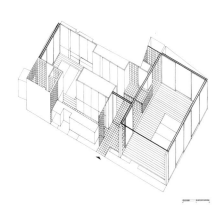

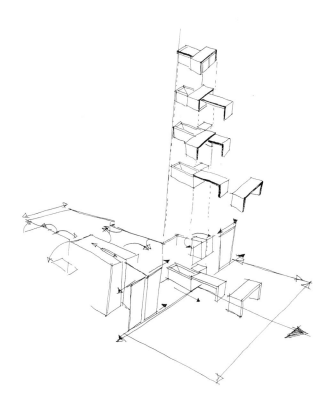

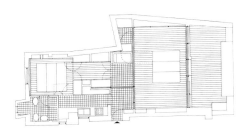

Helmut Dippold

Haus Ziegelberg

Bavaria

Haus Ziegelberg, a collaborative project between architects Helmut Dippold, Jeurgen Seeberger GmbH and interior designer Susanna Riede, was completed in 1999, four years after its inception. Inspired by a period spent loft-living in New York, Dippold approached the project for a family home in Bavaria with an idea for an open, spanning structure, divided with modular, flexible and rotating partitions that could be interchanged, removed or added in response to changing domestic requirements. This, he felt, was the 'modern form of living', due to its adaptability in a fluctuating urban and social environment. Through discussion, an even more flexible organism was born, which not only responded to the free-flow of family events, but also to the surrounding landscape and environment.

In plan and section a 'liquid space' contracts and expands through the main body of the house, defining the main living areas. On the ground floor, this weaves between and around the dining room, study and kitchen, which can open and close to varying degrees for incorporation into the main and infinite route pattern. The first floor is more clearly divided into south (family-orientated) and north (guest-orientated) bedrooms and bathrooms.

The jagged gash between is reinforced, but not formally dictated, by a regular cut of south-facing rooflights above, which spans the length of the building and directs light through the double-height space to the ground floor. The first-floor rooms are more conventionally sealed off from the gallery access with side-hung doors. Dippold describes the rooflights as a 'glass sculpture', an element that re-emerges vertically at the east end of the building to form the 'glass prism' of the living room. This angular protrusion oversails the lower ground floors (containing gym and swimming pool) and sits like the prow of a boat, jutting over the land that drops steeply away beneath it. The assemblage of differing facade elements of the house is designed to express externally the fluidity of the house's internal configuration. A smooth, curving, whitewashed, render wall contrasts with the timber-clad balcony area on the south elevation, which is scored with a regular rhythm of windows. The undulating sculptural surfaces play against the flatness and simplicity of other planes, just as the free design of the ground floor draws strength from being set against the more conventional planning upstairs. Dippold has achieved a practical and imaginative response to creating an adaptable house, which is arguably more individual and site-specific than the loft solutions that initially inspired him. ◌ *Sally Godwin*

Opposite
Haus Ziegelberg, Bavaria, 1995–99: external view, evening.

Above
Haus Ziegelberg, Bavaria, 1995–99: external view.

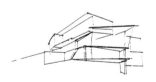

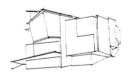

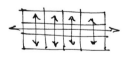

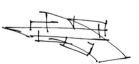

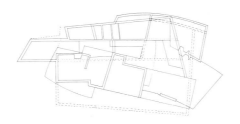

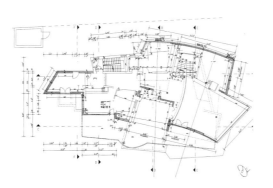

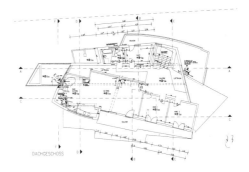

DACHGESCHOSS

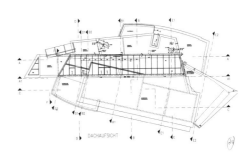

DACHAUFSICHT

Opposite top
Haus Ziegelberg, Bavaria,
1995–99: internal view,
roof light.

Opposite bottom
Haus Ziegelberg, Bavaria,
1995–99: sketch of design
progress.

Above
Haus Ziegelberg, Bavaria,
1995–99: internal view, stair.

Right
Haus Ziegelberg, Bavaria,
1995–99: plans.

BUILDING IDEAS

A small, London-based practice, Mark Guard Architects is well known for its elegant, functional, modernist house designs. Since its establishment in 1986, a pragmatic belief in working closely with clients and the pursuit of architectural ideas through the act of building has led Guard to explore transformable space. In the following interview, Helen Castle finds out how Guard first became engaged with the transformable and how, over time, he has expressed it in his built work.

New House in Galway, Ireland, 1992
Situated 4 miles from Galway city, in a rural setting, this house takes the vernacular exterior form of a traditional rural Irish building. The internal arrangement is, however, less conventional. On the ground floor are the children's bedrooms, overlooking the garden and connected to a basement playroom. The living-room terrace is connected to the garden by means of an external staircase, reminiscent of local barns.

Right
The Roxby House stands in sharp contrast to the region's adopted vernacular.

Above
View through the first floor of the house showing the living room opening onto the terrace, which leads to the garden.

Helen Castle How did you start formulating your own particular notion of transformable space?

Mark Guard Well, I guess it all began in 1986 when I bought a small property, and like most architects, demolished all the walls to make a big, open space. Then, of course, people wanted to come and stay and it's difficult if you don't want to sleep with them. I started thinking of ways that one could have open-plan yet allow for putting people up.

Then there was the frustration with London planning departments, which insisted on family housing. This was at a time when housing for single people was needed – families were breaking up and people were either living on their own or with a partner. Councils, however, continued to have an agenda about family housing. A large proportion of any development had to be given over to family housing – in some cases all of it. As a young person, who was aware of what was available to rent or live in, it seemed to me that this was going in the wrong direction. The demand was for smaller spaces in the city. One of the ways of dealing with the planners was to make accommodations that could be transformed to create a single person's flat with lots of space.

The other interesting development was the loft. Clients wanted the big empty space that they had bought as a shell, while also requiring individual bedrooms – their teenage son was going to visit them at weekends and where was he going to sleep? How was this going to work? If you started to include bedrooms, you knew the clients weren't going to get what they had bought. They would get a fairly ordinary flat. This encouraged us to think about new ways of putting these ideas together and trying to make an open-plan apartment that could be cleverly subdivided by the occupiers when necessary. The same applied to people who were working from home, who wanted a flexible working-living space.

Another factor in all this was the increasing cost per square foot of living space. People can't afford to buy the 3,000-square-foot apartments that ideally they would like; instead they buy one of 1,000 square feet, and then try to live in it as 3,000 square feet. This requires an approach to space that employs 'tricks', or an element of illusion.

At Bankside, you did this by stacking the guest bed above the bath and the other bed above the dressing area.

Yes, but the illusion of space was largely created by keeping the ceiling planes running through, and retaining the full dimension of two walls. It's extraordinary the difference you can make to space by having uninterrupted wall and ceiling planes.

Didn't you really start changing things around before that at Kensal Rise?

At Kensal Rise, we created flexible space through the use of conventional doors, just by having doors that could operate in two positions. The transformable space was in the planning – in the layout, if you like. We allowed for quite simple devices, such as doors to make the bedroom have no bathroom, or one bathroom *en suite*, or two bathrooms *en suite*.

When I worked for bigger offices – for Richard Rogers and Rick Mather – I got used to some of the technology that comes with larger scale buildings. In the faculty buildings at East Anglia, for instance, we had fire doors in the corridors to separate the building into compartments. The doors were held open on electro-magnets because you didn't want them to swing all day. The doors are released when the alarm goes off to create the fire seal. It seemed to me that we could take this straightforward, ordinary building technology and apply it to people's flats and houses. It seemed everyone was doing houses using the standard products and materials. They were tweaking them a bit, but they weren't taking what was available in the building industry and putting it into domestic architecture.

You've developed your own vocabulary, particularly with boxes and sliding doors, and especially in the bathroom.

There are two aspects to this. The first is this idea of taking technology and using it: you take doors, find out how they're held open, how they can be released, how they can go from floor to ceiling, how they can pass the fire regulations and all that stuff. You have to then consider how to take it further and make the space really work to achieve more than one expects. The influences here, I suppose, are mostly Le Corbusier – his sculptural forms, his willingness to bend a wall and play with the light, to create a special place. The boxes are part of that sculptural language. This has a great appeal to me, because normally in a room you're surrounded by walls, and the walls contain you. It's interesting to have an object in the room that isn't an object in the sense of being a piece of art or a piece of furniture – it's an object that is doing something. So it's maybe the side of a bathroom, part of a kitchen or a staircase.

Bankside Apartment, London, 1997

This flat was created out of a shell unit in the Manhattan Loft Company's Bankside development, whose exteriors and foyers were designed by Piers Gough. Though the ceiling heights were not high enough to accommodate two storeys, the clients required two bedrooms. Using the normally wasted space under the bed, sufficient height was created to allow for a dressing room under the master bed and a second bathroom under the guest bed. The long vistas of the main living area and the inclusion of sculptural volumes increases the sense of space.

1. Main living area showing large sliding door leading to the bed area.
2. Detail of steps up to master bedroom, concealed behind large sliding door.
3. Master bathroom, with circular WC cubicle.
4. Raised guest-bed platform.
5. Raised master-bed platform above wardrobe area.

A creative form, I suppose?

Or maybe it's a facade. At Bankside, the intrusions in the space, or what some might call 'installations', are like objects. They're not forming the boundaries of the room; they're forming something within the room that you look beyond and around.

Creating the art object in the landscape ...

Yes. And it's the idea of connecting people. We all live such artificial lives, so you have the thought of going home and retreating to your monastery, everything being very pure and empty of all the things that have caused problems to you during the day. But there's another way of thinking about it, which is the complete reverse: you go home and you're connected to the real world; you're connected to a more fundamental life. We need to be reminded that we're spinning around in that huge, strange infinity we don't understand. Thinking of it this way means that when we go outside, we walk into the artificial urban environment, where we have to deal with bosses and deadlines and things that perhaps don't have much to do with our existence on this planet. So rooflights, windows, controlled views and methods of dealing with natural light in your home environment, I think, can do quite a lot for people. It's quite a different feeling walking into something where you've been able to play with light from the sky as opposed to walking into an apartment that has a solid concrete ceiling. You're just left with what light you get through a window.

I suppose your ideal in a way would be the house in Deptford, because you have the garden inside and that's the ideal scenario because you have light coming in and lightwells all around.

Yes, it enabled us to play with the division between inside and outside, in the way that we talk about a room not having a defined boundary. At Deptford, we went to a lot of trouble to get all the windows and doors so they would disappear completely. When you look out, you're confused: are you inside or outside?

So that's the ultimate transformable space?

I don't think we've got there yet, but the inside/outside confusion will be important.

In the BBC Modern Times documentary about the house in Deptford, the couple who lived there used it almost as an art gallery.

They're extraordinary, because they really do want to change it, if not daily, at least weekly. They want to change some of the furniture around and adjust it, and they get pleasure from opening all the windows up even if it's a cold day – and then saying, 'Gosh, it's cold!', and closing it all down again. But a lot of people haven't really got that love affair with their home. They come in from a really hard day and ...

They just want to sit down on the sofa and relax.

When people come in really tired in the evening, we can give them an environment with a bit of sun coming in, hitting a wall in a certain way – a kind of connection with the outer world beyond and the sky. (You can obviously do that better with gardens and outside spaces.) The problem with the loft revolution is that there's no requirement for lofts to have outside space. Some have terraces, but the majority of people are effectively forced into boxes.
They may have high ceilings, but often there's no decent view, no rooflights, no cross ventilation, just a big box. It's not healthy. Part of the reasoning behind the modern movement and the clearing away of housing that was dark and dank and deadly was hopefully getting some light and air.

At Kensal Rise, you addressed that. You really opened up the Victorian terrace, and you changed what was a conventional plan. A lot of people in England still want to live in terraced housing, but you responded to changes in living and completely opened it up and turned it around.

Kensal Rise is a difficult one because while that's true, we created out of a four-bedroom house a house with one-and-a-half bedrooms plus a bit of study at the front. In return, however, they did get all that wonderful space. The most important thing about that house is the two staircases, because it means that you can basically do a circuit; you don't have to go back on yourself. One of the problems with the terraced house is the single staircase – it doesn't allow you to vary your route. When I was a student in Canada, one of the houses we rented had a back staircase, and I just thought, 'Every house has got to have one of these'. The tutor would come round to give me a review; I'd hear him at the front door and I'd be off down the back staircase! It was a great house to live in as the second staircase allowed for surprising encounters – you never knew where anyone else would be.

1 STUDY/ OFFICE
2 MEETING AREA
3 VOID
4 MASTER BEDROOM
5 STEAM ROOM
6 W.C.
7 BATHROOM
8 BED 5

1 ENTRANCE HALL
2 DINING
3 KITCHEN
4 LIVING
5 SHOWER ROOM
6 UTILITY
7 BED 2
8 BED 3
9 BED 4

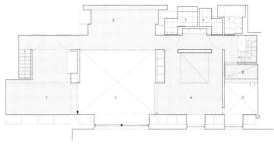

1

4

1 STUDY/ OFFICE
2 MEETING AREA
3 VOID
4 MASTER BEDROOM
5 STEAM ROOM
6 W.C.
7 BATHROOM
8 BED 5

1 ENTRANCE HALL
2 DINING
3 KITCHEN
4 LIVING
5 SHOWER ROOM
6 UTILITY
7 BED 2
8 BED 3
9 BED 4

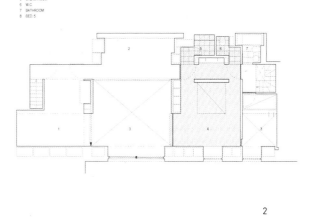

2

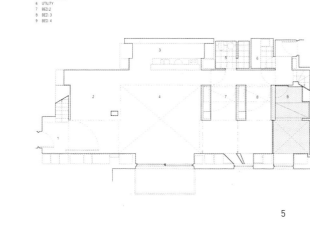

5

1 ENTRANCE HALL
2 DINING
3 KITCHEN
4 LIVING
5 SHOWER ROOM
6 UTILITY
7 BED 2
8 BED 3
9 BED 4

1 ENTRANCE HALL
2 DINING
3 KITCHEN
4 LIVING
5 SHOWER ROOM
6 UTILITY
7 BED 2
8 BED 3
9 BED 4

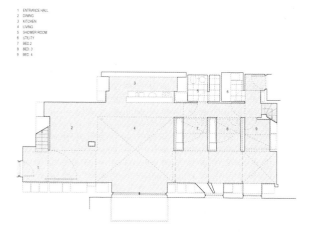

3

6

House at Deptford,
London, 1995
Created out of the shell of a
nineteenth-century, two-storey
coach house, this residence
was transformed from a
building with garage space on
either side into a house with
an internal garden to the right
and entrance courtyard to the
left.

Right
First-floor plan.

Far right
Section.

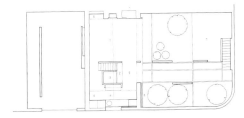
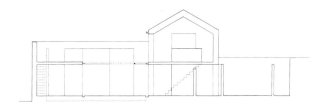

Opposite
Scheme for Apartment in
Piper Building, London, 2000
The client's brief for the
conversion of a 1,292-square-
foot loft apartment was to
provide five bedrooms, two
bathrooms and a study area as
well as the facility to use the
space for private photographic
exhibitions. From the entrance,
the view of the length of the
loft is maintained to maximise
the visual space. On the upper
level, the study area and the
master bedroom can be
opened up to the double-
height living room. A children's
study area is located on the
mezzanine above the kitchen
on the lower level. A number
of 'boxes' provide display
space for photographs. These
contain fold-down beds, and by
the use of sliding and pivoting
doors they can be transformed
into the children's bedrooms.

1. Upper-level plan in private
gallery configuration.
2. Upper-level plan configured
as a master bed area.
3. Lower-level plan in private
gallery configuration.
4. Lower-level plan
configuration: boys separate,
girls together.
5. Lower-level plan
configuration: boys away,
girls together.
6. Lower-level plan
configuration: one boy away,
girls together.

**The house in Galway must have been very
different from all your other work, as you're
generally associated with urban housing.**

It was difficult for us. The site was bought by the
client with planning permission for a bungalow.
It is also a planning requirement in that area
that all houses have to have pitched slate roofs.
We managed to build a four-storey house that
looks like a bungalow from certain angles.
Because it couldn't be exactly how we would
have liked, we took the traditional forms of the
Irish house – no overhangs to the roof, strong
gables – and then worked with these, really
perhaps more on the inside than on the outside.
It was in a way almost like a conversion job.
We were given this object, which is the shell,
and opened it up as much as possible. We put
the living room upstairs again. Like Kensal Rise,
it has a second staircase connecting down to
the garden, though outside on the gable. It's
an interesting house because although it's four
storeys, including the basement and the attic,
none of the stairs are in the same position.

**So you can't go from bottom to top on the
same staircase?**

You have to go up one staircase, then move
around a bit to find the next staircase to go
up to the next level, and then go across and
around a bit to find the next one. They're all
in reasonably close proximity to one another.
It gets you away from the continuous staircase
that just connects one level to another. There
was a lot of baggage with that project. Ireland
has something of a difficult recent history in
rural housing. Everyone wanted bungalows in
the 1960s, Spanish haçiendas in the 1970s and
the dreaded Neo-Georgian look in the
1980s. There was an agenda for the house in
Galway to try to get back to traditional proportion
and still achieve a modern, open house. It has
concealed sliding doors so you can subdivide
it into different spaces inside, or you can leave
it open. The nice thing is that our clients use
the doors and change the plan, closing it down
in the evening.
When we first built the house in Orme Square

in 1990, for instance, nobody used the huge sliding
doors that closed the living room off from the double-
height space. Now, as the kids have grown, those doors
are in use all the time – to cut out TV and stereo noise.
Originally, the doors were almost taken out of the
project, as the clients couldn't see the point of them.
For the first five years of the house, they weren't used,
but now they're in full-time use.

Do you live in a transformable way yourself?

Yes, I'm very lucky. I have two floors, one of which is
transformable and the other is a top-lit, open-plan
space. The transformable floor serves multiple
functions – study, dining room, laundry and guest
bedroom. I can create either one bedroom for a guest,
or a completely self-contained guest apartment.

**You seem to be responding to a change in living
patterns rather than imposing them. That seems
quite a conscious decision.**

We don't want to impose. Maybe that's every architect's
statement, but the client is very important. What the
client wants makes the project interesting. It's the
resolution of their disparate requirements and then
having to reshape their requirements into something
that will hopefully be aesthetically pleasing that is the
challenge.

**Your plan for a flat in the Piper Building is an example
of that, because your client's got four children. She's
a mother who wants working space and she also
needs to accommodate certain pieces of furniture;
also within that the children have got desks. It's very,
very particular.**

It's a very nice project and our client is great. She sees
no problem in asking for five bedrooms in a space
intended for a one-bed layout.
It can take time to find a design solution. However,
projects where you have to try and accommodate five
bedrooms yet maintain the idea of one large space,
become really interesting. Having faith in the design
means we know that it won't feel cluttered at the end.
We're confident that you'll walk into the apartment
and think it's quite big, and you won't really notice
all these five bedrooms that fold out of boxes and do
various things. ◭

**House refurbishment,
Kensal Rise, London, 1994**
In an attempt to create more
flexible and open space in
this typical Victorian property,
Guard inverted the plan of the
conventional terrace house.
On the ground floor are the
study and bedrooms, which
are interconnected by doors
that allow the occupants to
rearrange the extent of the
rooms. On the first floor is
the living room, kitchen and
dining area, which are opened
out to the garden by means
of a double-height window
and back stairs.

Right
The rear elevation is almost
fully glazed, exposing the
interior at night.

**House in Orme Square,
London, 1990**
Conceived as a modernist
reinterpretation of a London
town house, this project
maximises space, keeping it as
open as possible on the most
public ground and first floors.
Children's bedrooms and
bathrooms are on the second
floor. The open-plan master
bedroom is on the third floor.
All internal doors are full
height and are painted to
match the walls. The doors sit
in recesses in the walls and
are held open by floor-
mounted and wall-fixed fire-
door controls. Guard adapted
the type of electromagnets
commonly used for fire doors
in public buildings. These are
linked to a smoke detection
fire-door system, which
activates and closes the doors
in the event of a fire. Each
door is switched so they can
be closed individually if
required. The result is an
apparently doorless interior.

Right
Axonometric showing the
winding metal stair and the
double-height kitchen space,
which can be closed
off from the living room by
means of sliding partitions.

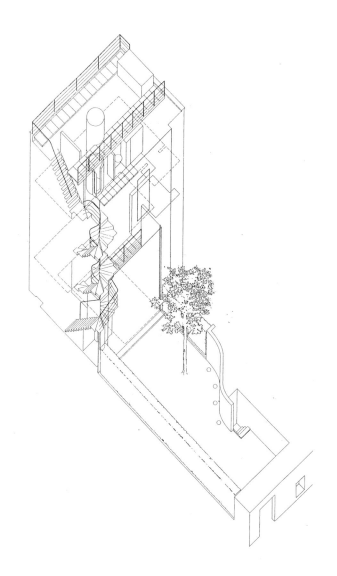

**The Transformable Apartment,
Soho, London, 1996**

The transformable apartment in the Manhattan Loft Company's Soho Lofts building represents one of Guard's more extreme developments of the transformable idea. Here, the apartment can have no bedrooms, one bedroom or two bedrooms, simply achieved by swinging large doors out from the freestanding boxes in the centre of the space. The beds pivot out of the boxes once the doors have been positioned to form the bedroom walls. The boxes also enclose the bathroom, while additional swinging planes provide an access corridor to the master bedroom when the guest bedroom is in use.

Right
Axonometric showing movable partitions.

Far right
Transformable configurations.

Below
General view showing kitchen open.

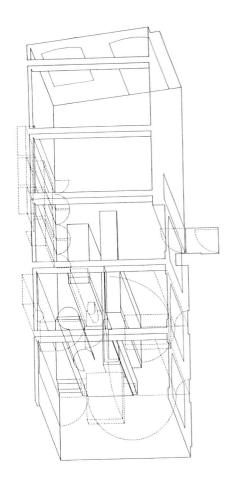

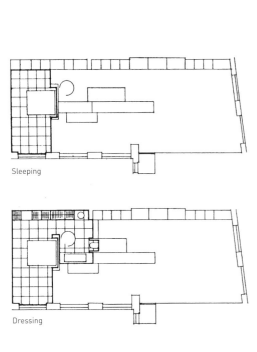

Sleeping

Dressing

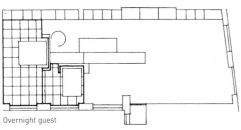

Overnight guest

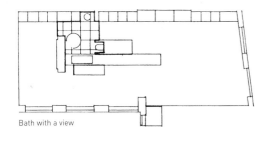

Bath with a view

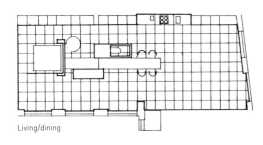

Living/dining

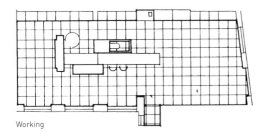

Working

Cartwright Pickard

Murray Grove Flats

Opposite
The main stair drum is
dramatically illuminated at
night, providing a focus for
the road junction.

Above left
Detail of the main facade. The
building has been robustly
detailed, and the duplication of
basic forms never becomes
repetitive or dull. (format:
transparency)

Above middle
The L-shaped building
overlooks a private courtyard
at the rear, with individual
balconies for residents.

Above right
The flats under construction,
showing the ease with which
each unit was craned into
position.

Notes
1 Keith Blanshard, Director
of Yorkon, quoted in
Architect's Journal,
17 February 2000, p 49.

Descending from cranes upon the traditional east London landscape of surviving terraces and uninspired high-rises at the end of 1999, Cartwright Pickard's Murray Grove flats caused a flurry of media attention. Together with Shepheard Epstein Hunter's Stonebridge Estate, London (1999–2000), this project has made a timely reassessment of the nature of building high-volume, low-budget housing developments in the UK, during a period of great strain on the housing market. Working in assocation with one of the oldest philanthropic housing associations in the UK, the Peabody Trust, Murray Grove is credited as the first large-scale, prefabricated housing scheme in the country. Alluded to in the media as 'pods', the flats at Murray Grove were prefabricated, complete with windows and doors, each brought to the site on a flat-bed lorry from a York factory. The ready-built units were stacked in two 'wings', spreading outwards from a central, circular staircase core, which was constructed in the conventional way.

British architecture's lengthy association with prefabrication has been surprisingly unfruitful. Despite the call in the golden age of modernism for 'machines for living in', the logical association with the manufacture of that other complex, mass-produced consumer object – the motor car – has never been consummated. Although the trailer home, the Portakabin and the flat-pack home (as typified by IKEA and Phillipe Starck, amongst others) have struggled to make a case for prefabrication (sometimes successfully, in countries like Sweden and iconic schemes like the Japanese capsule hotel), the sleek, injection mouldings envisioned by 1960s visionaries like Alison and Peter Smithson with their one-piece plastic bathroom for the house of the future, have singularly failed to materialise in concrete form, or in any other material for that matter.

Aesthetically, the scheme is light modernism, perfectly expressive of its factory-built origins and suitable for the need to transport the units by road. This also dictated size, as each unit – measuring 8x3.2x3 metres – could not exceed the maximum size transportable without the need for an escort. Built in collaboration with a Japanese company and a sub-division of Portakabin, the raw units were clad in terracotta tiles. The approach resulted in a swifter construction time, and site disruption was kept to a minimum. 'Next time, we would fix balconies in the factory', the head of the construction company was quoted as saying.[1]

Murray Grove was also experimental in the sense that it tried out technologies and processes for the first time. The attention it garnered in the architectural world (the flats have won an American Institute of Architects Award as well as being selected for the Millennium Products), led to government attention – a return to the glory days of old? ⌂ *Jonathan Bell*

Tillman Architects

Clifton
Gardens
Apartment

Small-scale domestic projects are by their very nature 'transformable'. From the outside, this stucco-fronted suburban London villa is indistinguishable from its neighbours. Inside, however, is another story. The owners of the property employed Tillman Architects, a small modernist firm based in central London, to address the lack of space and light, a common problem in cramped Victorian flat conversions. Keith Tillman, the project architect, describes his role as 'pushing, stretching and kneading' the interior of the two-storey basement and ground-floor apartment into a space that 'caters for modern-day living'.

After removing existing partitions and gutting the interior, the number of bedrooms was reduced from five to three. The wasted space generated by the old circulation areas was reclaimed and integrated into the living spaces. New circulation areas had to be multifunctional, reflecting different uses and configurations, and helping to preserve space. The glass staircase, designed in collaboration with structural engineers Alan Conisbee & Associates, illustrates the emphasis on dual function. Descending from the entrance hallway to the basement living area, the staircase serves as the means of access between the two floors and allows light to flood in and illuminate the basement space. In cross section, the glass appears thin and light, almost verging on the flimsy, while the elegant treads are unhindered by visible mechanical fixings. The lightly sandblasted steps are firmly slotted into the wall at each end, supported by a 3-metre glass beam. Careful lighting gives the glass a golden glow rather than the normal green hue. Whereas the previous staircase was a purely functional enclosed metal structure, this has become the focal point of the apartment, a place where one can appreciate the full width and depth of the house.

The *en suite* bathroom in the upstairs bedroom is designed as a freestanding installation. The great flat planes of sheer enamel-backed glass walls continue the feeling of space and the long lean lines that echo around the flat. These glass walls carry reflections from the trees and the garden on to the bedroom walls, yet they stop just short of the ceiling to create an illusion of an isolated area flowing into the larger volume of the space beyond. The second bathroom has three large pivoting doors, which also function as movable walls, enabling one to open up the bathroom into the bedroom.

Tillman's interest in intricate spatial arrangements extends to the lower floor. The downstairs corridor, for example, can be transformed into an enlarged bathing area, simply by swinging the large pivot doors to the wc and bathroom out into the corridor. These doors are designed to double as partition walls, bolting onto the facing wall, effectively enclosing and transforming a section of the corridor and creating a whole new room. The entire apartment can be redefined at will by giant floor-to-ceiling doors. At between 10–12 feet tall, the doors hide their monumental size when open by fitting flush to the wall, held in place by discreet electromagnets and concealing, when required, everything from whole rooms to small storage areas. ◐ *Jonathan Bell*

Opposite
Internal glass stair.

Top right
Bathroom.

Bottom
Kitchen.

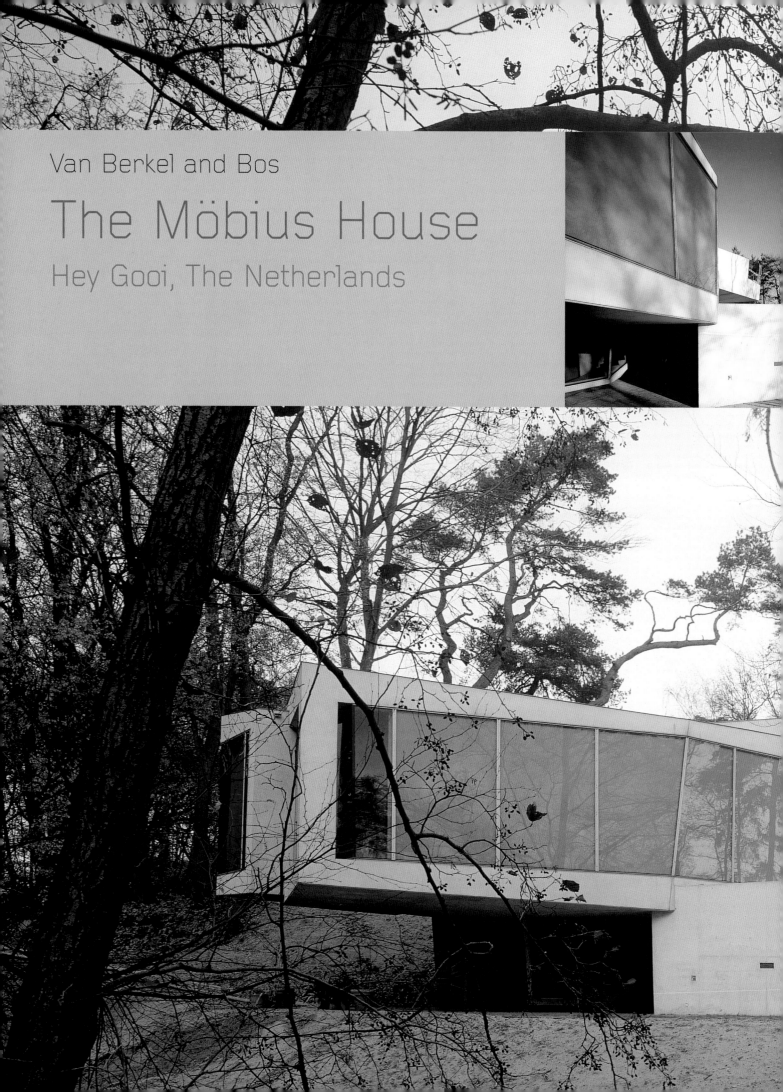

The Möbius House

Van Berkel and Bos

Hey Gooi, The Netherlands

As its name suggests, the Möbius House was inspired by the endless
loop or the möbius strip, 'a one-sided surface formed by joining
the ends of a rectangle after twisting one end through 180 degrees'.
This house could also be described as a multi-möbius strip, since
the narrative underlying its planning was a kinetic diagram
representing the trajectories of two individuals' life patterns,
intertwining and working against each other. At points, they meet,
and at these instances shared spaces are formed. Basement,
ground floor, first floor and roof garden: the journey of the house
interweaves with, and cuts, the ground line.

The play between folding and overlapping planes of concrete and glass creates a skewed, angular formality at the Möbius House that comes as a surprise given the organic diagrams that underlie the project. Van Berkel and Bos saw the concept of the generating diagram not as a restrictive principle, but as a means to free the architecture. Glazed partitions wrap round to become external walls; concrete construction folds to create useful excrescences; hanging concrete boxes form floor slabs, or stairs, and small pieces 'break off' to create hovering concrete furniture. The aesthetic is stark yet crisp, interjected at intervals by the introduction of richer patches of materials, like a deep-coloured wood for a ceiling.

Not surprisingly, the plan of the house is complicated and somewhat confusing to read, with walls and open spaces often difficult to distinguish from each other. This is not a static plan, reinforcing the fact that the ramped and stepped journey through the house is of the utmost importance and that experience is ultimately the best way through which to understand the Möbius House. The interior plan draws in references from the 2-hectare site in which the building sits, which has been divided into four distinct areas, each linked to the internal organisation of the house. The intention is to make the trip through the house simultaneously a walk in the landscape. The architects recognise the importance of the collaborative participation of the engineers, landscape architect and client in the evolution of the Möbius House: a constantly evolving journey that draws its inspirations from the routes taken in the daily routine of life. ◌ *Sally Godwin*

Previous spread
Möbius House
Het Gooi, 1993–97:
external views.

Right
1. Second-floor plan.
2. First-floor plan.
3. Ground-floor plan.
4. Basement plan.

Below
Concept sketch.

1

2

3

4

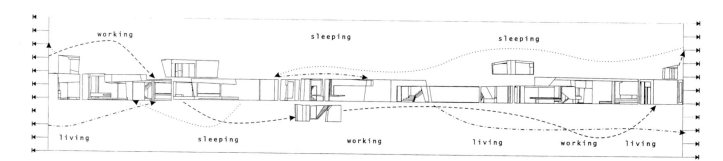

Stephen Varady

Perraton Apartment
and Measday Residence

Stephen Varady is an architect, writer and teacher. Since forming his own practice
in 1987, he has chosen to explore solutions to urban living, examining ways in which
spaces in the city can be made to feel larger and more expansive. Varady's approach
draws inspiration from many sources, including the work of Gerrit Rietveld and
the art of Kasimir Malevich. His 'kinetic' architecture creates an endless parade
of compositions and configurations, each carefully composed of elements within the
living space.

Previous page
Measday Residence, Woolahra, 1995
Interior, closed.

Above
Measday Residence, Woolahra, 1995
Interior, open.

Right
Perraton Apartment, Sydney, 1992
1. Bedroom, closed.
2. Bedroom, open.

1

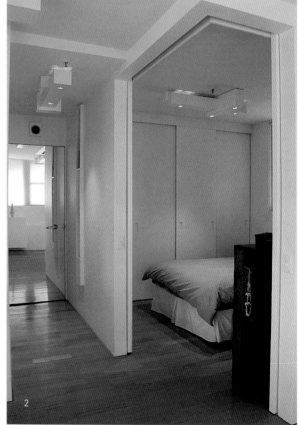

2

3

4

The Perraton Apartment in Sydney, 1992, illustrates this approach, with a folding dining-room table, a track-mounted television, a kitchen concealed behind a sculptural wall panel. The arrangement of sliding doors and walls means that, according to Varady, ' the design is never fixed – never static'. Bedroom doors slide open at 90 degrees to each other, opening up what was previously a corner. The elements of the concealed kitchen create an informal series of compositions, inspired by Malevich's Suprematist experiments in the interwar years.

The Measday Residence, 1995, a project for the extension of a terraced house in Woolahra, developed Varady's kinetic architecture. With a brief demanding a space that could be tightly controlled due to the exposed nature of the site, the solution was to provide a series of walls incorporating sliding partitions, be they of wood, glass or louvres. In this way, the living space could be opened into the rear courtyard, becoming an outdoor space in itself. Externally, wooden louvres create a street facade that can be altered to admit light or create privacy. Varady stresses the urban location of the project, and how this has acted as a catalyst for the exploration of these transformable themes. He speaks of the integration of kinetic elements into architecture, essentially in the same manner in which elements of surprise and delight are designed into consumer goods such as automobiles, elevating the functional into the fantastical and adding a layer of discovery into the domestic interior. ⌂ *Jonathan Bell*

5

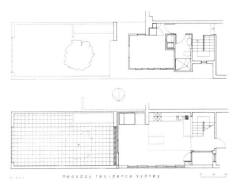

measday residence sydney

Right
Perraton Apartment, Sydney, 1992
3. Kitchen, closed.
4. Kitchen, open.
5. Kitchen, open (detail).

Far right top
Perraton Apartment, Sydney, 1992
Floor plan.

Far right bottom
Measday Residence, Woolahra, 1995
Plans.

Softroom

Projects for *Wallpaper** Magazine

Softroom's first major project was a short-listed scheme for the ill-fated Cardiff Bay Opera House competition. The firm (then comprising Oliver Salway, Christopher Bagot and Daniel Evans) used computer-generated visuals almost exclusively, not shying away from creating often outlandish and eccentric proposals for future living. By utilising rendering software to describe the living environments of the future, and realising them in a slick visual style that glosses over the technical limitations of contemporary building technology, Softroom makes futuristic projects appear practicable. These are schemes that draw upon science-fiction and architectural influences to provide desirable, if not achievable, spaces.

Sliding Block Hotel, 1998:
Above left: configured as a honeymoon suite.
Above right: configured for a meeting or as a remote office.
Below: plan configurations.

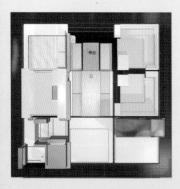
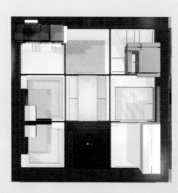
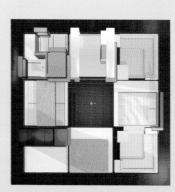

Floating Retreat, 1997:
helicopter pilot's view.
Beach view (inset).
Deck view.

In September 1997, Softroom began a collaboration with *Wallpaper** magazine, providing an illustration for a speculative Floating Retreat. It was billed as 'your own private tow-away desert island, complete with inflatable beach'. The magazine acknowledged that 'the first prototype would of course be quite expensive, but as a mass-produced product it would probably cost about the same as a medium-sized yacht'. Neatly tying in with the magazine's forward-looking editorial slant, as well as its almost obsessive attention to detail, the firm went on to present several more lifestyle-orientated virtual projects for *Wallpaper**, each presenting transformability as a natural component of contemporary living space.

The Floating Retreat was designed to be towed to a lonely atoll, preferably by a sleek powerboat. The carbon-fibre pod could then be inflated, James Bond style, creating an instant desert island paradise complete with all the urban mod cons the self-contained beach hopper would ever require. It was not, the magazine, stressed, at all the same as caravanning.

A subsequent project, the playfully titled Maison Canif, July 1997, was both a humorous rejoinder to the portentous nomenclature of the modern movement, and a spirited late twentieth-century response to the 'plug-in' architecture of Buckminster Fuller and his 1960s devotees. Food preparation areas, a sofa, bathroom and a bedroom could be swung out from a 'vacuum-formed titanium', penknife-shaped module, which was designed to be installed in redundant office space: an instant domestic transformer. The various combinations of the furniture and fittings could all be stored and recalled at the push of a button, much like the seat preferences in an executive saloon car.

Perhaps the ultimate experiment in life style transformation was the Sliding Block Hotel, which debuted in the April 1998 issue of the magazine. The almost childlike simplicity of the concept – a hotel room conceived as a sliding-block puzzle – allowed for massive permutations of space. Providing a meeting room, honeymoon suite, private gym or simple sleeping area out of a basic grid plus eight movable modules was an attractive, if far-fetched, idea.

Other Softroom work for *Wallpaper** included a Pantonesque private jet fit-out, and a project for the ultimate tree house (first, find the ultimate tree!) – diverse ideas that reflect the magazine's eclectic remit. The mixture of slick, rendered imagery and esoteric design solutions sets these projects apart from their proto-high-tech antecedents, both in terms of execution and style. That they exist at all is perhaps testament only to the demands of the magazine market. This might be reason enough to consider them as entirely symbolic of a new form of futurism, a futurism that considers technology to be a liberating creative tool that can transform, if not our actual environment, then our understanding of its potential. ⚙ *Jonathan Bell*

Maison Canif, July 1997
Top
Bathing area.

Middle and bottom
View of living area.

Right
Plan view.

Hans Peter Wörndl
The GucklHupf

Transformation in architecture need not rely on shifting use or reconfiguration. The architect Hans Peter Wörndl demonstrated a different commitment to kinetic space in his GucklHupf project, a 'folly' in the traditional sense, which stands at the intersection between form and function. The GucklHupf draws its strength from proximity to, and distance from, architectural syntax – ironically, the very ambiguity that led to its demise. Wrangles with the local authorities in the Austrian village of Mondsee over the exact status of the structure after the end of the festival for which it was built, eventually resulted in its removal: it had been deemed a 'building' and was therefore illegal under current regulations.

Plans   Sections

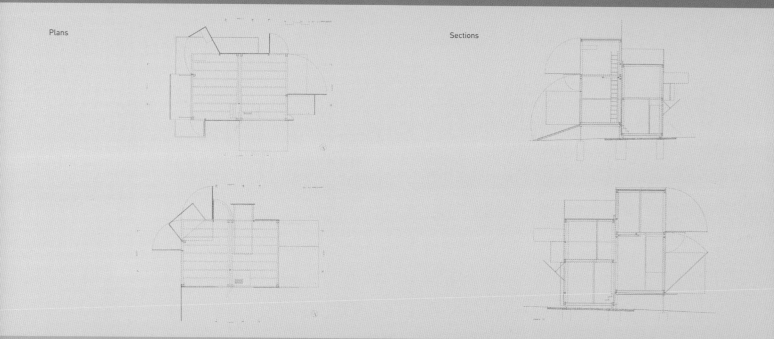

GucklHupf was built for the Festival of Regions in 1993 as one of a series of exhibitions, workshops and installations responding to the theme of 'strangeness'. Although the construction shares its name with an Austrian Sunday pudding, and makes reference to a nearby hill called the Guglhupf, more directly the title derives from the contraction of the two verbs *gucken* and *hupfen* – to watch and to hop. Passive and active, the name serves to reinforce the dichotomies that underlie the project: strange and familiar, habitation and travel.

On one level, the construction stands as metaphor for the house, planned as a series of characteristic elements, rooms and furniture. But this is an animate house, intended to 'live' after completion, with additional contraptions enabling the structure to open itself gradually into and against the environment in which it finds itself. This automated movement in

response to localised weather conditions was never realised, but by hand-activating the sliding, tilting and turning mechanisms attached to mounted plywood panels, the windowless box dissolved in infinite variety, at once framed in the landscape and framing it.

GucklHupf represents the disintegration of the conventional cocoon of the house, exposing the heart of the home to the 'outside'. This reinforces an understanding of the vulnerability of the thinness of external protective walls and, with its raised form and solitary nature, speaks of the architecture of travel and the mobile home. Similarities have also been drawn between this structure and the boat- and bathing-houses indigenous in the area.

In fact, the GucklHupf was open to a variety of non-domestic uses during the festival due to its transformability. Ultimately, one of the redemptive plans for the project was to airlift it to an alternative site by helicopter, but the project, in disassembled form, still awaits replacement. ◭ *Sally Godwin*

Richard Murphy Architects

The rapidly increasing demand for housing has made it imperative that we discover new ways of reusing existing buildings. In Britain, architects are stuck between a vociferous heritage lobby and the pressing need for new accommodation, a situation that has not always led to satisfactory solutions for the country's many thousands of important and derelict buildings.

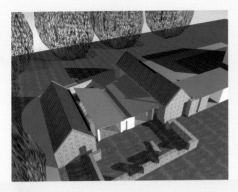  

Opposite top
**House extension,
Dirleton, 1999-2000**
The kitchen, viewed from
the garden. The long kitchen
windows pivot upwards,
creating a broad open space
that brings the garden into the
house. The extension
is constructed in modest,
vernacular materials, echoing
the existing house. The seven
pivoting window units are
sturdily framed and follow the
curve of the kitchen counter.
At the interface of the garden
and the new extension the
corner windows slide open,
creating an internal/external
space. A simple chain replaces
the conventional downpipe,
irrigating the garden and
providing a symbolic link
between the building and
its environment.

Opposite bottom
Royal Mews, Edinburgh, 1996
Exterior view showing the
large sliding door, which
evokes the former industrial
use of the building.

Top
**New House,
Broomhill (CAD) 1999-2000**
The existing farmhouse
'frames' the new-build
component: a glassy pavilion,
situated in the former
farmyard, which provides
a link from the old to the
new. The stone walls of
the existing building have
been accommodated by the
lightweight new insertion,
rather than suppressed by
an overbearing new building.

However, there are signs of a new approach.
Edinburgh-based practice Richard Murphy
Architects has become adroit at approaching
tricky buildings and sites, preserving the
elements that imbue them with character while
at the same time reordering and transforming
the internal space in order to accommodate
changing uses and requirements. One of the
practice's earliest successes was the
reconstruction of an Edinburgh mews. The mews
house, a building type that typifies the necessity
for a constantly adaptive approach to urban
architecture has seen a massive change in
fortune. From their original use as stabling,
mews have become some of the most highly
desirable addresses in Britain. Murphy's
transformation, which won a RIBA Award in 1996,
pivots on the insertion of a new floor level,
clearly indicated externally by the presence of a
steel beam which also functions as the runner
for the sliding garage door. A new rooflight
brings daylight down into the tall living spaces,
while the project also involved designing
furniture and fittings, transforming the
previously derelict building into both a vibrant
new home and an overall work of art.

The romanticism of ruins frequently offers
strong arguments against their regeneration
and reuse. When heritage organisations spend
vast sums re-engineering crumbling castles
in order to fix them for ever in a moment of
deconstruction, it is hard to imagine ruins ever
being recycled into contemporary dwellings.
A recent RMA project, the New House, 2000,
however, does just that, by taking a single storey,
stone, eighteenth-century Lothian steading,
and incorporating it into a new private home.

Readjusting the existing wings of the former informal
farm courtyard by the insertion of a new centre pavilion,
Murphy has bridged the gap between old and new.
Existing window openings are largely reused, and
the extensively glazed central pavilion acts as a
'hinge' – a new living area from which the older,
stone and slate parts of the building can be seen.

Maggie's Centre, a cancer information and
counselling centre at Edinburgh's Western Central
Hospital, took the aesthetic of domestic renewal into
the context of a small-scale medical building, creating
a human and domestic environment. The building is
spatially transformable, allowing it to be opened up
for larger sessions, or closed into smaller volumes
depending on need. The centre's success has led to
the practice being asked to rearrange and expand the
original scheme, 'pulling' the interior of the original
building out into an extruded extension.

Extending existing buildings is another area in
which architecture has traditionally been given a
chance to prove itself. Whether by juxtaposition,
homage or continuation, the character of extensions
is indicative of a practice's working approach. In 2000,
at a small ninteenth-century house in Dirleton, Murphy
demolished the existing extension and replaced it
with a slender addition containing a nursery and
new kitchen. Rietveld-inspired opening windows
characterise the gentle curve of the kitchen bay,
described by the architect as a 'console', which allows
one to feel that one is in the garden while preparing
food, washing-up, etc. The interface between house
and extension is signified by the use of white render,
while the extension seamlessly leads into the garden
space through the integrated wooden corner window-
seat and the chain-link drain, which draws rainwater
off the roof and back into the garden. ᴆ *Jonathan Bell*

Biographies of contributors

Jonathan Bell is a freelance writer and journalist based in London. He studied illustration and design history at Winchester School of Art. He has since contributed to *Wallpaper**, *Blueprint* and *Graphics International*, and is currently co-editor of *things*, a design history journal.

Iain Borden is Director of Architectural History and Theory at The Bartlett, University College London, where he is Reader in Architecture and Urban Culture. He is the author of *Architecture in Motion: Skateboarding and Urban Experience*, and, with Jane Rendell, of *DoubleDecker: Architecture through History, Politics and Poetics* (both forthcoming). He is currently working on an issue of *Architectural Design* with Sandy McCreery for the Summer of 2001, *New Babylonians: Contemporary Visions of a Situationist City*.

Catherine Croft is an architectual historian and writer. Previously an inspector at English Heritage, she is now Architectual Adviser to The Theatres Trust and Vice Chair of the Twentieth Century Society.

James Gallie works with Long & Kentish architects in London. He has written dissertations on Hassan Fathy's housing for the poor in Egypt, the politics of self-help refugee housing and a thesis entitled 'The Memory of Place – refugee shelter and settlement in Palestine', based on research in Gaza and the West Bank.

Miles Glendinning is head of the Threatened Buildings Survey at RCAHMS, Edingburgh.

Co-author of various books on Scottish architecture and the city, including *Clone City* (1999), *Home Builders* (1999) and *History of Scottish Architecture* (1996).

Sally Godwin studied architecture at Cambridge University and in 1998-89 she was co-editor and distributor of *Scroope 10: Cambridge Architecture Journal*. Currently, she works as an architectural assistant for Penoyre and Prasad Architects in London. She is also a researcher on Dennis Sharp's forthcoming publications.

Stefan Muthesius teaches at the World Art Studies Department, University of East Anglia. He is author of numerous books on architectural and urban history, including *The English Terraced House* (1982); a history of the new universities movement is forthcoming.

Dennis Sharp is a senior partner of Dennis Sharp Architects, London and Hertford. He was Editor of *AA Quarterly* and *World Architecture* and, from 1968–82, was Senior Lecturer at the AA. A professor at the International Academy of Architecture, he has taught at Columbia and Adelaide Universities and at UCL. He is currently preparing a new edition of *20th Century Architecture: A Visual History* and a monograph on Connell, Ward & Lucas.

Catherine Wood is a freelance writer on twentieth-century and contemporary art and Curatorial Assistant at the Barbican Art Galleries. She is also involved in 'seams', an anti white-cube collaborative installation project involving graphic designers, set designers, lighting designers and musicians.

Edited by Helen Castle

Critical Modernism
in the Twentieth Century
(as if Morality Mattered)

With the exciting new update of his 1969 book, *Architecture 2000 and Beyond*, now out, Charles Jencks places himself in an uncomfortable hot seat. How many of the predictions and prophecies that he made for the millennium 30 years ago have been fulfilled? How many of the shifts and turns in the architectural world were foreseeable? An essential overview of the previous century is provided in the book in the form of a new diagram, the Evolutionary Tree of Twentieth-Century Architecture, which maps architecture's continual revolutions in style. Here, he uses the same diagram to tell a new and freshly developed story – a story of 'Critical Modernism', the constant dynamic of dissent – which makes sense of the continual turmoil, divisions and diversity of twentieth-century architecture.

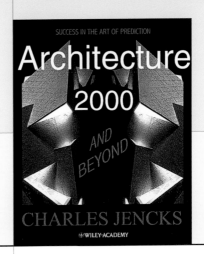

SUCCESS IN THE ART OF PREDICTION

Architecture 2000
AND BEYOND

CHARLES JENCKS

WILEY-ACADEMY

The Modern Movement was born and raised on a strict regime of moral crusading. Henri de Saint-Simon, in the 1820s, defined the role of the avant-garde as a kind of militant priesthood that would lead society in a progressive, scientific and artistic direction. Only the best, most progressive artists and architects, he wrote, could exercise 'over society a positive power, a true priestly function, and [march] forcefully in the van of all the intellectual faculties, in the epoch of their greatest development! This is the duty of artists, this their mission'.[1] A few members of the avant-garde took up Saint-Simon's call to arms and acted like 'the new priests' of a secular society: John Ruskin, Frank Lloyd Wright, Walter Gropius, Le Corbusier, Piet Mondrian, Constantin Brancusi and, more recently, Joseph Beuys, Louis Kahn and Daniel Libeskind. Even those who did not espouse an explicitly spiritual message, such as Joseph Kosuth or Aldo van Eyck, couched their ideas in highly moral tones – if not that of the priest, then that of the judge. And moral pronouncements issued continuously even from those, like Peter Eisenman, who were against an ethical system. Twentieth-century architecture was played out, verbally at least, as a morality play of heroes and villains.

Realists, of course, argue that this was just self-interest and that what was really at work behind the rhetoric was the first principle of architecture – 'get the job' – and the second – 'keep it'. But this cynical view may itself be blinkered. Maybe there was something going on underneath, to which the rhetoric referred, if only obliquely. Sigfried Giedion, in Space Time and Architecture, refers to the constant attacks on 'sham architecture' by Hendrik Berlage, Henry van de Velde and William Morris that have echoed through the Modern Movement.[2] The only problematic aspect to these attacks is that while the moral theme is constant, the meaning of what is 'sham' continues to change with regularity, as style and philosophy change.

An evolutionary chart of twentieth-century architecture (overleaf), which I first made for the book Le Corbusier and the Continual Revolution in Architecture, helps reveal this continual turmoil. The diagram shows 60 or so architectural movements, over 400 architects who made things change, and 100 events and outside forces that impinged on architecture. Although in my book I emphasise continual revolution, there are several different conclusions that can be drawn from the same diagram. I have also used it to tell other stories – for instance, in the recent update of Architecture 2000 and Beyond, to check how many predictions made in 1969 came true 30 years later. Here, I want to bring out what is a hidden truth of the twentieth century: the unlikely idea that morality plays a creative role in architectural history. It is unlikely because even idealistic accounts of twentieth-century architecture have to acknowledge the bigger context: the two world wars, fascist and corporate repression and today's immiseration of two billion people around the globe – not to mention ecological, urban and suburban horrors too well known to need repeating. Against these large and intractable forces, morality counted, and counts today, for little, and it has a marginal effect on things closer to home, such as mass housing, building codes, urban sprawl and any number of other important issues. How then, can a frail, marginalised and sometimes shrill voice have managed to make a difference? The answer turns out to be complex and indirect.

The first hints can be seen by looking at the basic narrative of the evolutionary tree, starting at the left. To make the point, I have exaggerated the following account and used green and red to bring out the heroes and villains – or rather, my personal view of them. Although this weighting reflects my prejudices, it is not without foundation.

A Personal View of the Twentieth Century

The twentieth century took off on a positive note with a strong, if not very vital, monumental classicism in the ascendancy – baroque in Britain, beaux-arts and urban in Europe and the USA. Its greatest practitioners were Daniel Burnham in America and Edwin Lutyens in Britain – the best of the 'sham architects' whom the Modernists were to attack. Challenging this tradition for supremacy were more creative movements: the Arts and Crafts and various forms of Art Nouveau and National Romanticism. Although these trends and schools were smaller than the dominant aesthetic, they were more visible and important. They addressed some of the key problems of the time, especially the cultural and symbolic ones, and produced unique urban masterpieces such as the Metro stations of Hector Guimard and Otto Wagner in Paris and Vienna, the Arts and Crafts Bedford Park outside London, and the brilliantly expressive public work of Antoni Gaudí, Louis Sullivan and Eliel Saarinen. The private houses of Victor Horta, Josef Hoffmann, Charles Rennie Mackintosh and Frank Lloyd Wright were equally dazzling and inventively made.

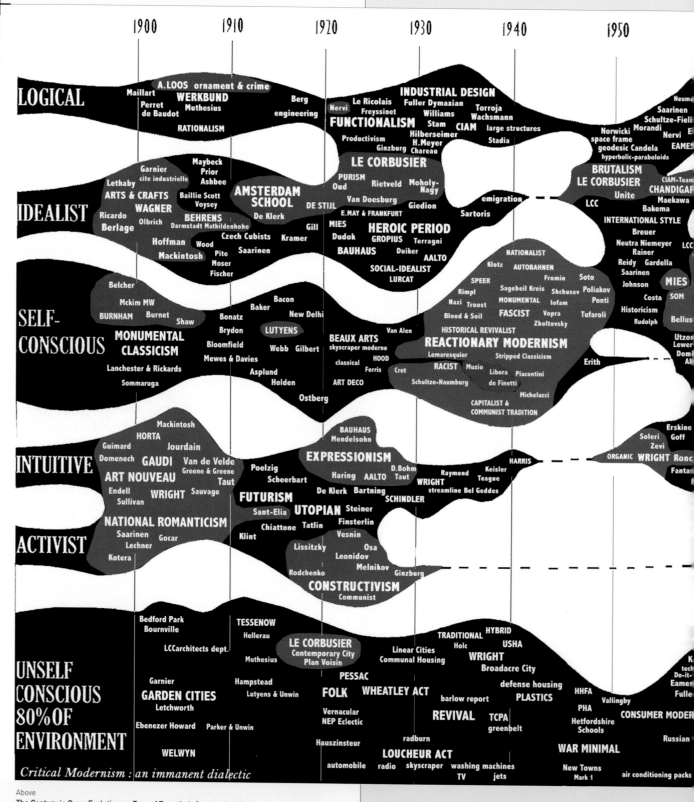

1900 **1910** **1920** **1930** **1940** **1950**

LOGICAL

A.LOOS ornament & crime
Maillart WERKBUND
Perret Muthesius
de Baudot
RATIONALISM
Berg
engineering
Nervi
Le Ricolais
Freyssinet
FUNCTIONALISM
Productivism
Ginzburg
INDUSTRIAL DESIGN
Fuller Dymaxian
Williams
Stam CIAM
Hilberseimer
H.Meyer
Chareau
Torroja
Wachsmann
large structures
Stadia
Neuma
Saarinen
Schultze-Fieli
Morandi
Norwicki Nervi E
space frame
geodesic Candela EAMES
hyperbolic-paraboloids

IDEALIST

Garnier Maybeck
Lethaby cite industrielle Prior
ARTS & CRAFTS Ashbee
WAGNER Baillie Scott Voysey
Ricardo Olbrich BEHRENS
Berlage Darmstadt Mathildenhöhe
Hoffman Wood Czech Cubists
Mackintosh Pite Saarinen
Moser
Fischer
AMSTERDAM
SCHOOL
DE STIJL
De Klerk
Gill Kramer
LE CORBUSIER
PURISM
Oud Rietveld Moholy-Nagy
Van Doesburg
E.MAY & FRANKFURT Giedion
MIES Sartoris
Dudok HEROIC PERIOD
GROPIUS Terragni
BAUHAUS Duiker
SOCIAL-IDEALIST AALTO
LURCAT
emigration
BRUTALISM
LE CORBUSIER
LCC Unite
INTERNATIONAL STYLE
Breuer
Neutra Niemeyer
Rainer
Reidy Gardella
Saarinen
Johnson
Costa
Historicism
Rudolph
CIAM-Team
CHANDIGAF
Maekawa
Bakema
LCC
MIES
SOM
Bellus

NATIONALIST
Klotz AUTOBAHNEN
SPEER Fromin Soto
Rimpl Sagebeil Kreis Shchusev Poliakov
Nazi Troost MONUMENTAL Iofam Ponti
Blood & Soil FASCIST Vopra Tufaroli
Zholtovsky
HISTORICAL REVIVALIST
REACTIONARY MODERNISM
Lemaresquier Stripped Classicism
RACIST Muzio
Schultze-Naumburg Libera Piacentini
de Finetti
Michelucci
CAPITALIST &
COMMUNIST TRADITION
Erith

SELF-CONSCIOUS

Belcher
Mckim MW
BURNHAM Burnet
Shaw
MONUMENTAL
CLASSICISM
Lanchester & Rickards
Sommaruga
Bonatz
Brydon LUTYENS
Bloomfield Webb Gilbert
Mewes & Davies
Asplund
Holden
Ostberg
Baker
Bacon
New Delhi
BEAUX ARTS
skyscraper moderne
classical HOOD
Ferris Cret
ART DECO
Van Alen

INTUITIVE

Mackintosh
HORTA
Guimard Jourdain
Domenech GAUDI
Van de Velde
ART NOUVEAU Greene & Greene
Endell Taut
Sullivan WRIGHT Sauvage
Poelzig
Scheerbart
BAUHAUS
Mendelsohn
EXPRESSIONISM
Haring AALTO
De Klerk Bartning
D.Bohm
Taut
Raymond Keisler
WRIGHT Teague
streamline Bel Geddes
SCHINDLER
HARRIS
ORGANIC WRIGHT
Soleri Erskine
Zevi Goff
Ronc
Fanta

ACTIVIST

FUTURISM
Sant-Elia UTOPIAN Steiner
Chiattone Tatlin Finsterlin
Klint Vesnin
Lissitzky Osa
Leonidov
Rodchenko Melnikov
Ginzburg
CONSTRUCTIVISM
Communist
NATIONAL ROMANTICISM
Saarinen Gocar
Lechner
Kotera

UNSELF
CONSCIOUS
80% OF
ENVIRONMENT

Bedford Park
Bournville
LCCarchitects dept.
Garnier
GARDEN CITIES
Letchworth
Ebenezer Howard Parker & Unwin
WELWYN
TESSENOW
Hellerau
Muthesius
Hampstead
Lutyens & Unwin
LE CORBUSIER
Contemporary City
Plan Voisin
PESSAC
FOLK
Vernacular
NEP Eclectic
Hauszinsteur
Linear Cities
Communal Housing
WHEATLEY ACT
LOUCHEUR ACT
TRADITIONAL HYBRID
Holc USHA
WRIGHT
Broadacre City
defense housing
barlow report PLASTICS
REVIVAL TCPA
greenbelt
radburn
WAR MINIMAL
New Towns
Mark 1
HHFA
PHA
Hetfordshire
Schools
Vallingby
CONSUMER MODER
Russian
K
tech
Do-it-
Eames
Fulle
air conditioning packs

Critical Modernism : an immanent dialectic

automobile radio skyscraper washing machines
TV jets

Above

The Century is Over: Evolutionary Tree of Twentieth Century Architecture. This simplified diagram is based on six major traditions of architecture (far left) that oscillate with respect to each other, like species. Green signifies my approbation, red my dislike, black a positive respect – that is, it is a personal, moral evaluation. About 60 explicit movements, or schools, emerged in the twentieth century and 100 or so social trends, new technologies and building types. In general, the evaluation of the significance pf the architects – about 400 of them – is based on consensus, although some judgements are arguable, such as the supreme importance given to Antoni Gaudí, and the presence of historians and critics who have formed opinion or theory.

The competitive pluralism – four to five movements at any one time and a new movement or trend every five years – is the engine of continual revolution. The dominant self-conscious tradition, first classical then Corporate Modern, successfully suppressed the power though not the influence of other traditions. Expressionist schools were born several times, never to become the mainstream, and the same is true of participatory design. Postmodernism, for a short time in the late 1970s and early 1980s, challenged its supremacy, but then became commercialised. Today, the Biomorphic School is a creative alternative to mainstream modernism, but it has yet to develop either the strength or following